# CONTEMPORARY PORTRAITS
(THIRD SERIES)

### BOOKS BY FRANK HARRIS

THE YELLOW TICKET

GREAT DAYS    A Novel

THE BOMB    A Novel

MONTES THE MATADOR

UNPATH'D, WATERS

THE MAN SHAKESPEARE

THE WOMEN OF SHAKESPEARE

SHAKESPEARE AND HIS LOVE    A Play

# CONTEMPORARY PORTRAITS

(THIRD SERIES)

By
FRANK HARRIS

GREENWOOD PRESS, PUBLISHERS
NEW YORK

Originally published in 1920
by Frank Harris

First Greenwood Reprinting 1969

SBN 8371-2577-4

PRINTED IN UNITED STATES OF AMERICA

## CONTENTS

|  | PAGE |
|---|---|
| INTRODUCTION | v |
| H. G. WELLS | 1 |
| UPTON SINCLAIR | 15 |
| JOHN GALSWORTHY | 31 |
| CUNNINGHAME GRAHAM | 45 |
| GILBERT K. CHESTERTON | 61 |
| ARTHUR SYMONS | 71 |
| WINSTON CHURCHILL | 87 |
| RUSSEL WALLACE | 103 |
| THOMAS HUXLEY | 115 |
| LOUIS WILKINSON | 131 |
| W. L. GEORGE | 143 |
| GAUDIER-BRZESKA | 149 |
| LORD ST. ALDWYN | 165 |
| AUGUSTUS JOHN | 181 |
| COVENTRY PATMORE | 191 |
| WALT WHITMAN | 211 |

# ILLUSTRATIONS

|  | FACING PAGE |
|---|---|
| H. G. WELLS | 1 |
| UPTON SINCLAIR | 15 |
| JOHN GALSWORTHY | 31 |
| CUNNINGHAME GRAHAM | 45 |
| GILBERT K. CHESTERTON | 61 |
| ARTHUR SYMONS | 71 |
| THE RIGHT HON. WINSTON CHURCHILL | 87 |
| ALFRED RUSSEL WALLACE | 103 |
| THOMAS HUXLEY | 115 |
| LOUIS WILKINSON | 131 |
| W. L. GEORGE | 143 |
| HENRI GAUDIER-BRZESKA | 149 |
| LORD ST. ALDWYN | 165 |
| AUGUSTUS JOHN | 181 |
| COVENTRY PATMORE | 191 |
| WALT WHITMAN | 211 |

# INTRODUCTION

WHAT a gorgeous undertaking it is to try to depict the soul of a man. A god-like hardship to render in words the utmost reach of thought and spiritual endeavor and the abyss of feelings, instincts, fears—the ghostly echoes in us of forgotten dangers or long disused powers. Of necessity the enterprise is a failure.

You might as well try to paint a wave and at the same time, its chemical constituents and its myriad animalculae.

You think of your friend's chief characteristic, the most prominent and peculiar trait of his nature and before you have got it on the paper, you recognize that he might correct you and declare that the opposite and antagonistic quality had guided him again and again and in fact finally determined his life's course.

Each one of us is made up of a myriad contradictories and no man has been able as yet to paint his own spirit in its entirety, let alone a stranger's, for we are all strangers one to another and lonely from the cradle to the grave, alone and forlorn.

Yet when we look at this impossible task in another light, it comes within our compass. If the complexities are infinite we have them all within us and so can piece out the portrait for ourselves. Moreover, if we are dealing with great men and their achievements our chief object should be to set forth the qualities and accidents that made their triumphs possible, for thus we render them comprehensible to others, an encouragement and perhaps an inspiration.

Great men are to us the ladder Jacob dreamed of reaching from earth to Heaven; they show us the way to climb, the heights to be reached, and are so to speak the altar-stairs of our achievement; the love of them a vital part of natural religion; their words our authentic inspiration and Gospel.

To know them by their works is not enough; we want the personal touch of intimate knowledge; the little vanity that acted as a spur; the trick of gesture or curious choice of phrase that throws light on some quirk of mind or idiosyncracy of thought. The works of genius will be there for men in the future to use and judge; the personalities should be preserved in the memories of contemporaries.

In this spirit I have worked and here they are my sixty eminent men pictured in their habit as they lived. In deference to our modern courteous custom I have extenuated a great many faults in my sitters, and assuredly have set down naught in malice. Indeed I have tried to paint no one whom I have not loved at some time or other and had the Age been less mealy-mouthed I should have liked to block in the outlines with heavier shadows and so reach a more vivid verisimilitude.

In my "Autobiography," however, I intend to be franker than the world will allow me to be in these "Portraits"; but I have no trace of malice or envy in me and accordingly shall always try my best to see my subject as he sees himself. For this is what we all desire, that men may see us as we see ourselves with a kindly eye for shortcomings and a mother's pride in our excellencies and indeed in our mere peculiarities.

The book as it stands is due to a remark Carlyle made to me once when he told me he had spent twelve— or was it fourteen years? on his half-hero Frederick.

"What a pity," I cried; "if you with your seeing eyes and painting phrases had only given us life-sized portraits of your famous contemporaries, how much richer we should have been. Had you only painted Coleridge, Lamb and Hazlitt, Thackeray and Dickens and Reade and Ruskin, Byron and Browning, to say nothing of Heine, Hugo and Balzac, as you painted Tennyson, what a gallery we should have had."

"May be," he said, "but I wasn't in sympathy with many you mention. Each man has to do his own work. Perhaps you will do portraits of your contemporaries and so fill the gap."

From that day on I kept it in mind as a part of my work and it is for others now to say whether I have done it well or ill.

Nine out of ten of these portraits have been painted with loving-kindness; if I find it hard to excuse the men who in stress of war gave up their opinions and turned their coats, or, if you will, yielded to popular clamor obeying obscure centripetal influences, my prejudice, if you will, or my sense of contempt is probably due to the fact that I have suffered all my life through unpopularity.

FRANK HARRIS,<br>
40 Seventh Ave.,<br>
N. Y.

H. G. Wells

# CONTEMPORARY PORTRAITS

## H. G. WELLS

WE all have our limitations, blind spots, shortcomings; we can all trace arrests in our development, knots which the sweet sap of life can hardly penetrate or vivify to growth; imperfections, not of the body or mind merely, but of the soul.

And these faults and flaws of ours prevent us from being faithful mirrors; this man we show well and that one badly, do what we will.

Often, too, the personage we ought to mirror best we do worst; people near us, like us, sympathetic to us, we cannot be just to, strain as we may.

And our blunders are incorrigible, inexcusable, inexplicable—loathsome to us as running sores, till we see that the greatest of men have to admit similar defeats. Then we resign ourselves:

"Why must I 'twixt the leaves of coronal
Put any kiss of pardon on thy brow?"

We men all need forgiveness: "pardon's the word to all," as gentle Shakespeare knew.

In my first volume of portraits I had to ask the readers' forgiveness for my poor, thin sketch of glorious Robert Browning.

Before I knew him I would have wagered that if there was one Englishman I could picture to the life, if I ever had the good fortune to meet him, it would be Robert Browning. Surely there was no fold, no corner, no innermost shrine in that spirit unexplored by my love! And yet, though I met him frequently, I could not get near him, could not even get him to sit for me.

In much the same way in this book I shall fail with H. G. Wells and the Devil alone can give the reason.

I find that when I say I discovered this genius or that, some of them resent it. Shaw said it seemed to him like patronage! Assuredly it was not so intended, indeed in my case was nothing more than the sad superiority of the senior.

Had I ever wished to make capital out of my personal relations with this or that man of genius I should certainly have published my reminiscences of Carlyle or Renan or Burton immediately after their deaths when curiosity was at its height and gossip about them universal. I could thus have won a cheap notoriety a score of times, but such vicarious limelight seemed to me degrading.

Wells, however, has since called me his "literary godfather"; admitted that I was the first editor to publish anything of his, so I may claim priority here even though it is only another word for chance.

When I took over the editorship of *The Fortnightly Review* Mr. Morley was very kind to me; towards the end of our talk he pointed to two large boxes in the corner of the long room and said:

"You'll find those boxes full of manuscripts: I ought

to have returned them long ago; some date back for years; some are recent. You could get your secretary just to send them all back and so be rid of 'em—the happy dispatch, eh?" And the bleak face lighted up with a glint of wintry sunshine.

With the conscientiousness of the beginner I went through the boxes. Ninety nine out of every hundred manuscripts were worthless; many out of date; some aimed at Morley's pedantic rationalism; only two struck me; one a story, the other a paper on "The Rediscovery of the Unique." The story and who wrote it I may talk of at some future time; now I am only concerned with the article. It set forth that the modern habit of generalization was an aid to memory but not to truth; the beads of fact we string together on one thread are all different. No two leaves of a tree are alike; no two eyes in a head are the same in shape or color; even the two sides of the nose are never exactly matched, nor the two lobes of any brain. Everything in nature and in life is unique, has to be studied by itself; for the soul and meaning of it is in its uniqueness and it will not yield its secret save to loving study of its singularity.

The paper was charmingly written, the style simple, easy, rhythmic; the architecture faultless. The signature surprised me. I had expected some well-known name: H. G. Wells!

"Have you ever heard of Wells?" I asked my assistant. He shook his head.

"You will hear of him," I ventured. "And now I want

you to write and ask him to come to see me any afternoon here!"

A few days afterwards Wells called and I asked him to take a seat I told him of his article and how greatly I admired it, all the while studying him. A man of middle height, well-made, with shapely head, thick chestnut hair, regular features; chin and brow both good; nothing arresting or peculiar in the face, save the eyes; eyes that grew on one. They were of ordinary size, a grayish blue in color, but intent, shadowed, suggesting depth like water in a half-covered spring; observant eyes, too, that asked questions, but reflection, meditation the note of them; eyes almost pathetic in the patience of their scrutiny.

His manner was timid; he spoke very little and only in response; his accent that of a Cockney. He professed himself a student of science.

"I've written some things for science papers, for *Nature*. I scarcely hoped to have this paper accepted; it has been so long since I sent it in. I'm glad you like it...."

He was so effaced, so colorless, so withdrawn, that he wiped out the effect his paper had made on me. I lost sight of him for some time, but knew his value.

When I took *The Saturday Review* I asked Wells to review the best novels for me. In the few years that had elapsed since our first meeting, his manner, I found, had entirely changed; there was no trace of timidity now; a quiet self-confidence had taken its place; the provincialism of accent had also disappeared. He was uncertain, he said, whether he could write regularly for me; "creative work is beginning to take up most of my time; still, I'd like now and then to say what I think of some good book...."

The first piece of journalism that counted was his memorable review of Conrad's first novel, "Almayer's Folly."

It sold out the edition in a week and laid the foundation of Conrad's fame—"broad bases for eternity," if only he had known how to make use of them.

Naturally I was delighted and gave Wells every opportunity of repeating his feat; but he had no other opportunity for triumph so far as I can remember.

I did not see much of him while he was working on the Review; but I found that he was scrupulous in keeping his word; his articles were always forthcoming at the time indicated and they were uniformly excellent.

One incident, however, impressed me peculiarly. Early in 1895 I brought out a volume of American stories: "Elder Conklin." I had had them by me so long in print that I had lost interest in them. As soon as a story appears in book form or in a magazine it never seems to belong to me any more; I am able to regard it then with some detachment almost as if another person had written it. I was leaving the *Saturday Review* office one day when I ran across Wells; he stopped me with a word.

"I have been reading that book of yours and wanted to talk to you about it," he began. "I had seen some of the stories when they appeared in *The Fortnightly* and liked them; but in a book the effect of them is altogether different."

"Really?" I questioned.

"Half a dozen stories," he went on, "give you an impression of the writer; enable you to form a judgment of him; whereas a single story or even two or three read at long intervals have not the same power."

"Curious," I interjected, "it is not quantity with me, but always some little intimate touch or piece of self-revealing that lets me see the writer's soul, and once I get the cue my impression is usually confirmed by his other writings."

"It was the whole book," he went on, "that gave me a view of your sub-conscious self. I call it sub-conscious because it is so unlike the Frank Harris one knows."

"I don't follow you," I said dryly.

"Well," he began afresh, "when one meets you, you are about the most dominant, imperious personality I've ever seen; but in this book one finds a modest, patient and peculiarly fair-minded person, who wishes first and last to present every one impartially and find some soul of goodness in every outcast even. I could not but ask myself: which is the real man?"

"Both," I replied laughing, and went my way. But Wells's insight had greatly increased my respect for his intelligence. It was the first time I had been so analyzed to my face and it gave me an odd shock that among these conventional, subdued, cautious folk I was regarded as a wild American, or what Shaw has since called "a ruffian."

Still, I consoled myself quickly: I knew how little manners count in the final estimate of a writer, less even than his personal appearance; it's his work alone that matters and by that alone he'll be judged. Who cares now that Shakespeare's manners were said to be "too sweet" or Beethoven's too insolent and domineering. Rebel or courtier, ingratiating or cynically contemptuous, no one will care which you were, ten years after your death.

On reflection the interesting thing to me was that Wells too wanted to see other men as they really are; he, too, was evidently trying as I was trying to get from the writing to the writer. The consequence was that I became interested in him, and read his first book carefully.

"The Time Machine" and other strange stories impressed me hugely; I thought them excellent; the best of their kind ever done; but I could not believe that such Jules Verne yarns would outlast the generation for which they were written, though Wells was a head above Verne both in content and handling: a born story-teller of the best with an imagination fecundated by scientific speculation.

A little later I read "Love and Mr. Lewisham" and found that I had underrated him; Wells might be a great novelist, might do something that would outlive his generation or even—

Filled with admiration I began a mental portrait of him and kept asking about his life in order to correct or confirm my deductions.

I found from a dozen indications that he was very touchy about his social position, anxious to be well up in the latest society slang, to dress and behave correctly.

When I mentioned this to some one who knew Wells intimately, he replied:

"Wells's father, you know, was a professional cricketer, getting in the summer months perhaps $25 a week. He has come from the bottom and learnt all the society touches as a man and is therefore naturally nervous: a little unsure of himself."

On the other hand I soon discovered that Wells had a curious conviction of his own greatness both as a writer and thinker; but especially as a thinker. His education was very modern; he had never been brought into close contact with the greatest minds in the past; he measured himself only against his contemporaries and thus found a thousand reasons to justify a high self-estimate.

Wells's first successes came to him when he was only twenty-nine and they were flattering enough to turn the steadiest head. His scientific stories had an extraordinary vogue, were translated into a dozen languages; by the time he was thirty-two or three, Wells was known from Kyoto to Paris.

And when he turned to writing novels of life and character his vogue helped him; the great wave of his popularity lifted him over one difficulty after another. While still a young man he was earning more than a Cabinet Minister and was received almost everywhere; listened to also by older men, men of established position, with a certain deference or at least with courteous attention. Women too made much of him; he is quite good-looking and intensely interested in the fair sex and as usual they returned that compliment with uncommon zest.

Now all this is infinitely pleasant to a man, intoxicating even; but it is not the fate Fortune allots to those rare spirits destined to steer humanity.

Cervantes lost the use of a hand in the battle of Lepanto; was taken by the Moors and worked for years as a slave; then in his native land when he managed to get a pitiful post he lost it on a false accusation and was again thrown into prison. Finally at sixty, poor, neglected, almost destitute with six women and several little children dependent on him, "in poor health and very anxious," as he himself said, he sat down to write "Don Quixote."

The great popular writer of the time, Lope de Vega, sneered at him and his works; declared that "Don Quixote" was poor, second-rate trash; used all his power and influence to crush the older man who wasn't even a rival but a belauder of de Vega's "most ingenious and interesting comedies."

Yet no one reads de Vega to-day and no one can avoid reading the comedy and tragedy of "Don Quixote," the greatest prose book in the world, I think, after the Bible.

But "Don Quixote" didn't assure to Cervantes his daily bread. Even after he had brought out the second part at seventy odd years of age he was poor and often in need. But his immortal courage never faltered. Just before his death the Bishop of Toledo wrote to him saying that he would like to help him if he wanted anything.

"Nothing for myself," he replied, "my foot is already

in the stirrup, but if your lordship would help my poor wife and her relatives, I'd go content!"

That's the sort of life men give to their teachers and true guides.

Success is its own handicap and nowhere in life except perhaps in politics is success so seductive as it is to the writer. Editors flatter, publishers offer golden baits, strangers enquire eagerly about the next book; fair women show impatience; what can a man do but write when writing comes so easily?

Alas! facile, fluent writing makes very hard reading. And the man who produces a couple of books each year should know that he is writing for the day and hour and is nothing but a journalist. Great work is not done at such speed. And Mr. Well's speed seems to be increasing; in 1918 I read "The Soul of a Bishop," and "God, the Invisible King," and "Mr. Britling Sees It Through." The two first quite unreadable, altogether unworthy of Mr. Wells's talent and position. "Mr. Britling Sees It Through" was dreadfully tedious for some hundreds of pages; but the last fifty or sixty pages redeemed the book.

And now this year I have had much the same experience: "In the Fourth Year," by Mr. Wells, is a mere pamphlet on the times and anything but a good pamphlet, while the long novel "Joan & Peter" deserves little consideration. The first two hundred pages of it are deadly dull and wholly uninspired; when the children grow up, however, the narrative becomes interesting in spite of being interrupted on almost every page by some remark on the war or comment on this or that phase of the struggle which is merely adventitious. The love-story with its touch of novelty in the boldness of Joan would have made an excellent short story. Mr. Wells has almost buried it in 500 pages. I do not believe that the next generation even will take the trouble to disinter it.

But all this matters little or nothing. A writer is judged by the best in him and not by his mistakes and blunders. His faults and shortcomings do not even enter into the account. The question is: has Mr. Wells written anything that must live; one masterpiece is enough for any man's measure. Surely the answer as yet must be in the negative. I don't forget "The War of the Worlds," or "The Time Machine," or "The Island of Dr. Moreau," still less "The Country of the Blind," or "The Research Magnificent."

But no one of these by any stretch of sympathy can be called a masterpiece.

Mr. Wells, however, has still time; I only regret that he has allowed these last four years with their insistent urge and appeal to drag him into journalism and pamphleteering.

But will he ever give now what we have a right to expect from him? I still hope or I shouldn't have written about him at this length. He began so well. In the famous nineties in London he was a prominent Fabian with Sidney Webb and Bernard Shaw. True, he left the Fabians rather rudely and drew down on himself one of the few contemptuous harsh letters which

Bernard Shaw has written. Since then he has caricatured Sidney Webb and his wife mercilessly; but all that is of small and transitory importance.

He may never write a great novel of revolt; yet may still have a great love story in him. It should not be difficult for him to beat "Tom Jones." He has a better brain than Fielding and a far more flexible style; knows women, too, if not men and criminals, better than the great magistrate. Why should he not write a novel that would stand to "Tom Jones" as "La Recherche de l'Absolu" stands to "Manon Lescaut"?

I should be more than hopeful were it not for his attitude on this world-war. For years he talked of imminent victory, vilified the Germans and exalted the British, with the myopic fervor of an Arnold Bennett. Now if one may judge by "Mr. Britling" he is slowly coming back to sanity again; but his recent laudation of "The League of Nations" is in the same overpitched key, almost hysterical, as far from sober reason as Kipling's crazy phillippics.

Again and again now in this way, now in that, Wells reminds me of Upton Sinclair. They are both healthy, and on the whole well-balanced, and yet endowed with extraordinary ability; they should both do great work and yet one gives us "The Jungle" as his best, and the other "The New Machiavelli," or "Mr. Britling."

It was bruited about in London at the time that "The New Machiavelli" derived its fervor from the fact that much of it was autobiographical. I am not especially interested in that view of the matter believing as I do that all the best creative work must necessarily be drawn from personal experience. The artist's task still remains to make what is individual, universal and thus give the mortal, immortality.

Wells has no doubt been run after by women and made much of by pretty girls; he is not only virile but good-looking and even in the early thirties was invested with the halo of fame. Moths flutter to the light, but when they give their bodies to be burned they diminish, for a moment at least, the illuminating power. In the case of an artist no one cares whence the inspiration comes; the fact of its presence is all-sufficient justification.

Mr. Wells is a far better writer than Mr. Sinclair, lives too, nearer the centre, is more exposed to high criticism, and yet he can write "The Soul of a Bishop" and "In the Fourth Year," and he is now well past fifty; still, while there's life there's hope.

Mr. Well's latest work, an attempt to write the natural history of the earth from the time it was thrown off from the Sun to the present, is ambitious enough in all conscience; but the great artist as a rule has enough to do to write the natural history of his own soul, leaving speculation about origins and developments outside himself to the camp-followers of science. He is a pioneer of the advance and is vitally interested in forming or heralding the future in accord with his own development leaving the dead past to bury its dead.

Upton Sinclair

## UPTON SINCLAIR

A HANDSOME fellow of good middle height and strongly made, Sinclair reminded me at our first meeting of Wells; but his features were even more regular and his forehead broader. The eyes, too, were fuller of light and kinder than Well's eyes; not such reflective mirroring pools, I mean, but quicker, brighter, vertical wrinkles between the brows—surely of doubt and thought; perhaps of disappointment grown impatient or querulous. Nevertheless, a fine wellbalanced face, backed by direct cordial decisive manner which contradicted the wrinkles.

Sinclair was still young—about thirty-two—and had already *The Jungle* to his credit and half a dozen other novels; he might well be one of the Sacred Band, seer at once and creative artist—another Cervantes. "The Jungle" was very nearly a masterpiece; if the end had been worked up crescendo to flaming revolt, it would have been the finest of American novels fit to rank with "Robinson Crusoe," "The Pilgrim's Progress," and "The Cloister and the Hearth." None of these books was written before the author was forty; what might not Sinclair do in another ten years? Clearly he was a man to know, worth careful study.

Unluckily for me he was then on his way to Holland, stopping in London only for a short time; he could not give me another meeting though he was kind enough to say that he regretted the necessity.

I talked to him of his new book, "Love's Pilgrimage," which I thought a mistake, and in the unexpurgated form, a blunder. There were fine pages in it, however; here and there an original thought; a mind beginning to feel its own power.

The book was so different from "The Jungle" that in spite of its shortcomings it testified to uncommon width of vision. I was eager to know how Sinclair had grown; what reading he had done, and what thinking to come to his power as a story-teller. For as Dante knew, the man who can tell convincingly what he has seen, must have a noble mind. Sinclair gave me the outlines of his early life quite simply: I reproduce his words:

"I was born in Baltimore in 1878. I went to the public school and the College of the City of New York, where I studied the things which interested me and neglected those that did not interest me.

"In the last year I got leave of absence for several months, stayed at home and read omnivorously. The three men who had most to do with the shaping of my thought were Jesus, Hamlet and Shelley. But at this time I also read and studied especially Carlyle, Browning, Milton and Goethe. Tennyson I read, but was always irritated by his conventionality. Arnold was, I think, next to Shelley and Shakespeare, my favorite poet. I loved his noble dignity—rather mournful—not at all what I was or meant to be, but the best of the old stuff.

I think a lot of Thackeray, too. I read all the Germans up to Freytag before I read any French, so the French had less influence on me. But Zola taught me a lot. I said of the "Jungle" that I had tried to put the content of Shelley into the form of Zola.

"I do not 'still' read Latin and Greek, as you suppose. I never read them. I studied Latin five years and Greek three years. I looked up some words in the dictionary ten thousand times and forgot them ten thousand times. I said what I had to say on the futility of language study as it is done in colleges in two articles which you will find in the files of the *Independent* along about 1902 or 1903. When I came out of college I taught myself to read French in six weeks and I learned more German in one month by myself than I had learned in college in two years.

"I did graduate work at Columbia University for four years. I began about forty courses and finished half a dozen of them. I quit because Nicholas Murray Butler fired all the men who had any life in them.

"My first short story was published when I was fifteen."

Sinclair appears to have read almost completely for pleasure and perhaps there is no better way. But when he says "all the Germans up to Freytag" he clearly means merely modern Germans and apparently is not a student. But I wanted him to tell me how his thought grew and the stages of it. How came he to see the vices of the individualist competitive system of our time and realize its atrocious injustice with the flaming passion that sears every page of "The Jungle"?

He replied frankly:

"What brought me to Socialism was more Christianity than anything else. I saw that those who professed Jesus did not practice him nor seem to understand him, I wanted to. And the more I came to doubt his divinity, the more important it seemed to me to understand and apply the human side of his teaching. I wrote 'Arthur Stirling' and 'Prince Hagen,' which are pretty much Socialistic works, before I ever met a Socialist. I thought I was the only person who knew those things; I had the burden of it all in my soul at twenty; and then, when I ran into Leonard Abbott and Wilshire I discovered it was all known before."

Sinclair did not feel as I did the necessity of embodying the two opposing principles of individualism and Socialism in life, and so I put the question to him: "Do you believe Socialism will supersede individualism? I want the state to take over many departments of labor; to resume possession of the land and to nationalize railroads, telephones and telegraphs, etc. I hope municipalities will take charge of all local public services; but you seem to want Socialism everywhere, seing no shortcomings in it."

Sinclair replied: "I have never doubted Socialism. You see I use the word in a broad sense to mean the change from private ownership and exploitation to social ownership and co-operation. As to ways and methods, etc., I have an open mind, and change it continually. I am a half-syndicalist, and I understand that the final goal is anarchy, so I can get along with all the sects. I think an open mind is my chief characteristic; at any rate my belief in it. I try to combine moral passion with good judgment, and I know it's hard to do because I see so few who even try it.

"I try to be impersonal; that is rather easy for me, because I am naturally absorbed in ideas. I prefer getting alone and reading about world events to meeting anybody. I naturally don't see people. I mean, I don't notice their eyes or hair, etc. . . . Sometimes I am rude without being able to help it, because I am easily bored and have great difficulty in controlling myself; I mean that my mind runs away before I know it and I am chasing some thoughts inside myself.

"I find that I have started out to tell you about myself as I really am, and as I suppose that's what you want, I'll go on.

"When I was young, eighteen or so, I thought I was inspired; at any rate I had some sort of a demon inside me and I worked day and night and ate myself up. I set out at seventeen to try and learn the violin, and I practiced ten hours a day, practically every day, for two or three years. I mean that literally; eight to twelve; two to six and eight to ten. Then I got married and had to work at things that carried at least a hope of money.

"I had supported myself by writing from the time I was fifteen. But when I got to be twenty (and had marriage in view) a desire to write serious things overwhelmed me, so I could no longer write the pot-boilers, dime novels, jokes, etc., by which I had paid my way through college.

"From twenty to twenty-six I nearly starved. All my novels of that time—'King Midas', 'Prince Hagen,' 'Arthur Stirling,' 'Manassas,' and 'A Captain of Industry'—brought me less than one thousand dollars altogether. I lived alone on $4.50 a week in New York and I lived in the country with my family for $30 a month. I really did it—had to. Hence my bitterness and my fury against poverty. They can't fool me with phrases.

"When I wrote what really interested me I never stopped day or night for weeks at a time. I mean that I had the thing I was writing in my mind every moment —I think even while I was asleep. I developed a really extraordinary memory for words; I never put pen to paper till I had whole pages off by heart in my mind. I would walk up and down thinking it over and over and it would stay in my mind—whole scenes.

"In the Stockyards I came on a wedding and sat and watched it all afternoon and evening, and the whole opening scene of 'The Jungle' took shape in my mind, and I wrote it there and then; I mean in my memory. I never jotted a note, nor a word, but two months later when I settled at home to write I wrote out that scene, and I doubt if three sentences varied. I can still do that. . . ."

At our first meeting we talked of a hundred things. It was evident at once that Sinclair had the heart of the matter in him—a passionate longing for justice and a better life for the mass of the people. I told him how greatly I admired "The Jungle" and how inevitable it was that it should catch on in England before it did in the United States and become infinitely more popular in London than in New York. The aristocratic class in Great Britain is fairly well read and has no sympathy whatever with the new-rich whether manufacturers, provision merchants or shopkeepers. Consequently they read of traders' crimes with delight and chuckled over the exposure of the nefarious methods of the meat-kings. Similarly a book exposing the stupidities of the feudal system with its hereditary powers and privileges would be pretty sure to take better in New York than in London.

"Your book is a great book," I said to Sinclair, "and there are more people in England able to appreciate high work than there are in the United States."

He agreed with this dogma a little reluctantly, I thought; but he did agree which showed extraordinary fairness of vision.

We parted regretfully and it was not till long afterwards I realized that I could not paint him because I had seen no shortcoming in him, no whimsies of temper, no limitation of insight, no lack of sympathy for any high endeavor.

For years now we've been in correspondence and since I've edited PEARSON's, Sinclair has written article after article for me and at length I'm able, I think, to trace the orbit of his mind. For if this war has done nothing else it has tested friendship and tried men as by fire; forcing them to reveal themselves to the very innermost chamber of the heart.

Moreover, I have now read all Sinclair's writings and I may as well confess it at once there's a Puritanism in him that I can't stomach and that, I believe, injures all his work. There is no passionate love-story in any of his writings. Take his latest work, "King Coal," which has just been published by Macmillan. In "King Coal" there is a superb Irish girl who confesses her love for the hero and offers herself to him only to be told by him that he is in love with another girl and engaged to her. There is no love-story in "Love's Pilgrimage," or in "Manassas" or in "The Jungle." Yet I have an unreasoned conviction that the greatest stories of the world are love-stories and no *Tendenz-Schrift,* no novel-with-a-purpose, however high, is going to live with the tale of Ruth or Juliet or Manon Lescaut.

In his essential make-up Sinclair is more like Arnold Bennett than Wells. Arnold Bennett, too, has never been able to write a love-story; but then he has not Sinclair's insight into social conditions, nor Sinclair's passion for justice. His shortcomings don't matter much while Sinclair's fill one with regret. So few are called to great work. Why will not Sinclair put his hand to the plow and give us the masterpiece we expect from him.

It seems to me that he may do this at any time. He appears to have all the powers necessary and he sees himself with the detachment of genius. The other day he sent me a eulogy of Jack London that I thought overpitched. I praised Emerson to him and Poe and Whitman in comparison, and in reply he answered me thus:

"I find London more interesting as a personality than any of the men you mention. Emerson is much nearer my own temperament because he had a Puritan conscience; but he was very apt to run to abstractions and to facile optimisms. . . . Poe had imagination without conscience. . . . Jack London was antagonistic to me in many ways but he had the eternal spirit of youth."

Excellent criticism this, though I don't agree with the classification; Emerson is among the world's thinkers, the greatest American after Whitman, whereas London in my opinion has done nothing that will live. But it is "the Puritan conscience" or rather the Puritan strain in Sinclair, thinning his blood, which I regard as perhaps his most serious limitation. Here again is his own statement on the subject:

"Some day I hope to write a novel; I don't know what the name of it will be, but in my own thoughts I call it my "Sex Utopia." I am going to try to indicate a solution based upon science and adjusted to the economic changes which I feel are pending."

I find in this last sentence the essence, the quiddity of Upton Sinclair. He would seek to solve even this problem with his head and not with his heart. Yet Vauvenargues found the supreme word when he said: "All great thoughts come from the heart." Now how would the heart solve this puzzle which arises chiefly from the polygamist desire of man?

It seems probable to me that the virginity and chastity of women will come in time to be less and less appreciated or desired. In this particular as in many others, the French appear to be leading civilization. At the bottom of their hearts they think chastity a matter of small moment (la rigolade) and they esteem free unions when they are serious just as respectfully as marriages. The Anglo-Saxons will of course demand definite instructions and for them the solution has already been indicated.

When George Meredith came before the problem he did not hesitate to advocate "marriages for a term of years, say ten, due provision being made for the children."

But Sinclair would have "a solution based upon science," even in a matter like this which is eminently an affair of the heart and only to be settled by each pair for themselves. But at his best he sees deeper. Here is his thought:

"I was brought up a Christian, and I followed the ascetic ideal until I was married at twenty-one. I have since come to think that ideal perverted; but on the other hand, I have seen so many deplorable results of promiscuous experimenting among radicals that I am very cautious in the ideas I set forth.

"I can not believe in the present institution of marriage-plus-prostitution. I do believe in early marriage, with divorce by mutual consent at any time. All of our thinking about sex must at the present stage of things be conditioned by the fact of venereal disease, which is so wide-spread, so subtle, and difficult to be sure about.

On this account any sensible person would wish to keep very close to monogamy.

"On this, as well as on higher grounds, I advocate very early marriage with the prevention of conception until a later period. This early marriage ought to be sensibly regarded as a trial marriage, and there should be no children until it was reasonably certain that the couple was well mated.

"Ultimately I look forward to maternity pensions, co-operative homes, such as I tried to found at Helicon Hall, and community care of children, which will relax the present strict family regime. I mean it will set free the parents from being slaves to their children. At present no intellectual people can have children unless they are very wealthy. I know many wretchedly miserable people who stay together on the children's account, and yet it doesn't really help the children who know their parents quarrel and learn to disregard both of them."

This statement seems to me full of interest yet unreasonably rational if I may so speak. I think the problem altogether too complex to be solved at this time; to attempt to solve it by "co-operative homes," seems to me amusing. Of course the community should be glad to take care of all derelict children, but most mothers would not willingly surrender their rights over their offspring. The main thing is now to make divorce as easy as marriage, and to be tolerant and sympathetic to all those who go their own way scorning convention and custom. But now to come to the question of the day:

Why does Sinclair take sides with the Socialists who

are in favor of prosecuting this unholy world-war with all vigor? He is, of course, a far abler man than Charles Edward Russell; far better informed too; yet he holds similar opinions. He is convinced that we must democratize Germany in some way or other; he has persuaded himself that the German cherishes dreams of world domination. He does not even rise to the height of the English socialists who declared the other day that no one nation was responsible for the war, that all the combatant peoples were equally to blame. He writes me that "if we had failed to combat the submarine threat, we should have made a blunder as tragic as if we had failed to support Lincoln in 1860, but I want to make clear that my militarism is only for the period before a German revolution; after that I am for a revolution in America and for nothing else."

My disagreement with Sinclair on these matters is fundamental; I want as many different forms of government as there are different peoples and different flowers in a garden. The genius of the Russian and perhaps of the German, is towards Socialism, as the genius of the Englishman and the American is towards individualism; why should any people wish to constrain another?

During the war our differences came to a break. Sinclair stated in his paper that Lincoln had abrogated individual liberty as completely as Wilson and had suppressed as many newpapers. I denied this and asked Sinclair for proofs. He wrote saying he hadn't the needful books at hand and after the war admitted that he had exaggerated.

Such a difference between us may seem small; but it is important I think. I believe that the force of gravitation operates on minds as on bodies; that the centre-seeking force acts in proportion to the mass and therefore I anticipated a vastly greater patriotism and impatience of opposition in 1917-18 than in 1863-4, and the herd-feeling showed itself almost to delirium. I thought it, therefore, the first duty of every able man to defend the liberties of the individual. I was hurt that Sinclair should have thrown himself madly on the side of the herd-instinct already far too powerful.

I have indicated such differences of opinion between us because in the main I am in profound agreement with Sinclair and recognize him as a lover of truth at all costs.

Take for instance his views on personal immortality; the subject Emerson would not discuss with Carlyle though he recognized their fundamental agreement. Here is what Sinclair thinks:

"My attitude is a peculiar one. I stopped thinking about it when I was seventeen, which was when I gave up calling myself a Christian. I have had only a mild curiosity about it since, because the present life is so intensely interesting to me. If the forces which gave me this life should see fit to give any more I will be pleased, but I do not hold them under any obligation to do so, and the probabilities look to me as if they would not do so. Of course we have to admit that there is a Divinity which shapes our ends because we are products of instinct, and our reason has been unfolded out of instinct, but I have the idea that reason is or will become a higher power than instinct. My religion is the religion of experimental science, which I believe will ultimately remodel and re-create all life."

Sinclair's view is nearly mine; but I have no interest in personal immortality at all. It seems to me a child's dream. I only wish I had realized earlier all one could do with this life and with oneself if only one had understood man's god-like power in youth. Goethe came near the truth:

> "Die Zeit ist mein Vermaechtnis
> Wie herrlich weit und breit.
> Die Zeit ist mein Vermaechtnis
> Mein Acker ist die Zeit"

But even Goethe did not tell us how glorious our inheritance was, how infinite our powers. We can shape ourselves into Supermen if we will, or better even than that; we are not only sons of man; but of God as well, and able to put ourselves into perfect relation with the Spirit that made the world and is still growing to its divine fulfilment. And as God one will be able not only to reveal hitherto undreamed of possibilities in the soul, but also exercise an influence which shall alter and beautify the earth-vesture of the Spirit in a way altogether incredible to us today. I believe that as we get better, we ameliorate unconsciously the climate and land in which we live. Blizzards and heat waves are leaving New York as we grow more humane, more considerate of others. The sunsets here are not so lovely as those of the Burgundian plateau because we are too heedless to love them as the French do; but our skies are illimitably higher here and the air ineffably lightsome because with all our shortcomings, and they are maddening, we have a loftier ideal and a more unselfish than any Latin people.

It will be said that I have fallen into transcendentalism and lost myself in imaginings but imaginative speculation is to writing what sky is to a landscape and I will not even beg my reader's pardon for the flight.

To return to Sinclair; I am not only in close agreement with him, but I have a very genuine admiration for his extraordinary talent. It is seldom that men admire those who resemble them closely. As Anatole France was fond of saying, "I must know all that my contemporaries are thinking so I never read them: they don't interest me."

I have over Sinclair the sad superiority of the senior: I am more than twenty years older than he is and so inferior to him as a younger-born of Time. He is not yet forty and when I think of all I have learned since I was forty I am ashamed of finding any fault in him; for in the next twenty years he may outgrow all his limitations and make my judging appear impertinent. But at the moment, sixty has perhaps some right to tell forty how to steer between Scylla and Charybdis between too little self-restraint and too tight a rein particularly if sixty is inclined as in this case, to advocate a more complete self-abandonment.

In my opinion "The Jungle" is so superb and splendid

an achievement that it justifies us in hoping even greater things from Upton Sinclair. His criticism, too, of others, is excellent; penetrating at once and sympathetic: he even sees himself with exceptional detachment and fairness. To set bounds to his accomplishment would be merely impudent; but I am sorry that he has written "King Coal" which is merely another Socialist novel.

Again and again I return to it: I wish he would fall desperately in love as one falls in love at forty when the heat of summer is still painting itself in gorgeous colors on every fruit and every leaf, making even the forest a flower-bed of indescribable richness and beauty.

He tells me he is married again and happy. In Pasadena he says the wildflowers are tinted like orchids and breathe forth an almost intolerable wealth of perfume. That's the place for this Emersonian. I want him intoxicated with the heady fragrance of love.

John Galsworthy

# JOHN GALSWORTHY: A NOTABLE ENGLISHMAN

JOHN GALSWORTHY began his literary work about thirty by writing a novel; in the next ten years he had produced three or four; I looked through one of them, but didn't think much of it; the feeling in it was not profound and the style meager -tame. In 1906, when he was forty, "The Man of Property" appeared, and about the same time a play of his, "The Silver Box," made a sort of hit. I read "The Man of Property," but it did not change my opinion materially, though it showed development. Galsworthy had taken the next step and now used an economy of means that betokened a mastery of his instrument.

There was a good deal of talk about him at this time and I gathered that he was a Devon man, belonged to the so-called upper middle-class and was fairly well-to-do. Suddenly, in 1910 I think it was, his play, "Justice," struck the nerves and drew the town. The piece was well constructed, that we had expected, and at the same time the morality of our "justice" was put on trial and our legal punishment shown to be tragic. With "Justice" Galsworthy came into the first rank of contemporaries, was now someone to know and watch.

I was not much in London at the time and we didn't meet. The other day I heard that he was to lecture in the afternoon at the Aeolian Hall, New York, and I went. The hall was more than half full—an excellent audience.

Galsworthy came to the platform in ordinary walking clothes, went over to the reading-desk, smoothed out his MSS. and began half to recite, half to read his lecture. He is about medium height, spare of habit and vigorous, his head long, well-shaped; his features fairly regular, a straight nose, high forehead; he is almost completely bald and wears glasses. His voice is very pleasant, clear and strong enough; he uses it without much modulation; gets his effects rather by pauses than by emphasis; has every peculiarity of the writer and not the speaker.

His essay dealt with the various elements of formative force in our civilization. It was interspersed cleverly with stories, not invented by the speaker, and I caught myself saying again and again half in approval, "how English he is and how pleasant!"

Then it struck me that if I could give Americans this mental picture of Galsworthy as an Englishman of the best class and an excellent specimen to boot, it might be interesting; do some good; at any rate the portrait would be worth doing. Accordingly, at the end of the first hour, I began to note what he said, or was it that about this time he began to say things that interested me?

He spoke of Bolshevism at some length and very sensibly, with infinitely more understanding, of course, than Senators Overman, Wolcott and Company, though without sympathy.

In the evolution of human society, he said, a revolt, and much more a revolution, was in itself a proof of injustice, of wrong done probably to the lowest classes, and of suffering brought upon the workmen and their families unjustly. Clearly the lessons taught by Carlyle have at length sunk into the English consciousness and tinged all thought.

Not a word did Galsworthy say about "outrages," of which we have heard so much from our lawmakers who are far too busy to restrain lynchings; but a caution against accepting glib statements of the press that were manifestly inaccurate.

The press, Mr. Galsworthy insisted, should be very careful to tell the truth and the whole truth, or its influence might be evil rather than good. Did he mean to hint that our American papers were more careless of truth than even English papers? I think he did, and as far as the "kept" press goes I believe he would have been justified in speaking his mind plainly.

But now to return to Bolshevism. It never seemed to occur to Mr. Galsworthy that the motive power of revolution might not be so much an uprising against injustice and a resistance of wrong as an attempt to realize a great hope, a resolve to shatter the framework of society to bits in order to remould it "nearer to the heart's desire." But if he had known Lenin or Trotzky or indeed any of the English labor leaders, such as Clynes or Thomas or Lansbury, he would have known that there is a new ideal abroad in the world and the hearts of men are thrilling with a glorious hope of ending or at least of mending this dreadful competitive society, all organized by and for individual greed where the many sheep are the prey of the few wolves, and injustice is built up to insane lengths by the principle of inheritance.

But your well-bred Englishman is always an upholder of the established fact, always prone to find virtue in whatever exists. He would make some man of property, some educated Sancho Panza his hero and the American, it now appears, would go even further and turn Don Quixote's idealism into comic relief or even confine the noble Don himself in some lunatic asylum or jail.

Galsworthy went on to speak of the League of Nations as another influence for good in our civilization, and here I confess his Anglicism surprised me. He declared very contemptuously that the League of Nations in his opinion was " a lost dog" save in so far as it was founded on Anglo-American unity. I simply gasped at this way of ensuring a world peace. And his English conception of democracy was just a little one-sided. "A democracy," he said, "like every other system of government, is there to pick out the best men and give them the greatest amount of power; in fact a democracy is there simply to affirm the true spirit of aristocracy."

It was plain that in spite of clear-cut phrases and the epigrammatic endings of not a few of his paragraphs Mr. Galsworthy was steadily losing his hold of his audience. The most English-loving Americans would hardly agree with this definition of democracy, and perhaps Mr. Galsworthy felt this, for his peroration was evidently designed as a sop to American feeling. With much earnestness, and Mr. Galsworthy is able to convey a great sense of seriousness and sincerity in his quiet way, he declared that the most perfect man, the greatest civilizing influence in four centuries, was—George Washington!—not Owen, or Fourrier, or Marx; not Goethe, or Lincoln, or Carlyle, no, Washington. And that was the end.

A day or two afterwards I had a talk with Galsworthy in his hotel.

Seen close to, his face becomes more interesting; the serious blue eyes can laugh; the lips are large and well-cut, promising a good deal of feeling, but the characteristic expression of the face is seriousness and sincerity.

I began by praising his insistence that a democracy as a method of government must be judged by its success in producing the best men.

"Still, that is not all the truth, is it?" I queried. "Surely the sense that the race is an open one and that we all have had a chance in it makes defeat easier to bear than when some person is put above us simply because he is the son of his father."

Mr. Galsworthy shrugged his shoulders; it seemed immaterial to him.

"Don't you feel," I went on, "that while there is a little greater love of freedom perhaps in England than in America, there is a certain sense of equality here that is unknown and unappreciated in Great Britain?"

He looked at me as if he hardly understood.

"I merely mean," I went on, "that the ordinary man in America is able if he gets an opportunity to speak to a governor, or senator or the President and shake hands with him, on an equal footing, whereas in England he would find that impossible with any person in authority. In fact, even the distance from Mr. Lloyd George, let us say, to Lord Lansdowne, is a very long one indeed."

"Well, perhaps," said Galsworthy, desirous of being fair-minded but unpersuaded.

I broke new ground. "Your praise of George Washington absolutely took our breath away. A good many Americans think Lincoln a far greater man, and I am afraid I share that view. How on earth did you get the idea of George Washington's greatness?"

"He did such great things," said Galsworthy, "and he remained so eminently well-balanced—so sane."

I could not help smiling: the English ideal of balance and sanity to be the measuring-stick of humanity.

"I'm just reading of Tom Paine," I said, "I cannot help thinking him a far bigger man than Washington. Perhaps it would do me good to write a eulogy of Washington and you a panegyric of Paine," and we laughed.

The talk wandered off to Ireland and Egypt and Mesopotamia. Galsworthy said that an American had told him that the poor people had never been so well off in Mesopotamia as since the English had come there: he thought that the fellaheen in Egypt had never been so prosperous as under British rule; but he was too fair-minded and truth-loving to delude himself with the same argument in regard to Ireland. He evidently believed that the failure of British rule in Ireland was an economic failure. He did not attempt to shut his eyes to the fact that the population of Ireland under British rule has shrunk from over eight millions to under four in less than a century. Still an Irish Republic seemed to him extravagant, almost absurd. He wanted to know why the Irish demands have increased. Why the Irish wanted Home Rule thirty years ago while today they want an Irish Republic?

I laughed. "I might say that it was a result of further experience of British rule," I replied, "but I do not think that. I think the difficulty is a little the Egyptian difficulty. Forty or fifty years ago the priests of Ireland used to be educated on the continent, at St. Omer in France. Now they are all educated at Maynooth and are merely educated Irish peasants. Formerly they had a cosmopolitan training which inclined them to tolerance of English ways of thought and feeling; now it is different: they are pure Irish."

Again Mr. Galsworthy's serious eyes brooded:

"I wonder why you don't agree with my view of a League of Nations?" he said. "It seems to me so plain that the peace of the world can only be kept by an Anglo-American alliance."

"What heresy," I cried. "I think that such a league would sooner or later provoke a counter-league of Russia and Germany and, perhaps, Japan and result in another world-war. I don't believe that Russia, Japan and Germany will ever accept British supremacy of the seas now that they have found out how vital it is to success in war. Do you think that Russia with 180,000,000 of people—a country three times the size of the United States and with almost double the population—will sit down for say a century to come in a position of absolute inferiority to England and America and accept their alien domination? The whole idea to me is insane.

"Like a great many others I dreamed of another League of Nations. I believed that Mr. Wilson would call the representatives of Germany and Russia to the peace table; and that he would begin by saying that here there was no conquered and no conqueror; that now the Germans and Russians had got rid of their autocratic governments the time had come to treat them as friends and equals and settle everything equally and justly— generously even. Lincoln would have done this. Now Austria is dismembered and starving: Germany maimed and mutilated: Russia attacked north, south, east, and west by her own Allies while the conquerors squabble and fight over the spoils."

The light died out of Galworthy's eyes. "We must agree to differ," he said drily.

The talk drifted to books and writers, and quite honestly I praised his "Justice," confessing that I preferred it to "The Man of Property," which seemed to surprise him. "There is infinitely more feeling in it," I said, "a passionate appeal to a higher justice than is to be found in English law."

"What a rebel you are!" he exclaimed.

"What are you now going to tell us about America?"

"I know so little," he replied; "I have been here only three months and I was here before in 1912. It is so hard to learn anything about it; it seems to be without marked features. How can an artist picture it?"

"Yet O. Henry did," I said.

"Yes," he admitted at once. "Yes, very interesting work his; very vital."

"And David Graham Phillips," I went on. "Have you read him?"

"No," he replied; "No, I think I have read one book of his; it didn't make much impression on me."

"Yet he is almost of Balzac's class," I ventured.

"Really," he cried in wonder; "really; you surprise me! I must read him. What are his best books?"

"I'll send some to you." I replied.

"That would be kind of you," he said, "and then: "What do you think of Masefield? I admire some of his work so much."

"I think him over-rated," I replied, "just as I think the war-poets altogether over-estimated."

"Did you like "Nan?" he insisted.

"Not particularly," I replied.

"Did you meet Masefield when he was in New York?"

"No, I had no wish to meet him. You know if you hadn't written "Justice" I probably shouldn't be here today. I look on 'Justice' as a great play: I put it with Hauptman's 'Die Weber.' I am grateful to you for it. Go on in that vein. What are you doing now?"

"Another novel," he said.

"Ah! I said, "I have always thought a new novel meant a new love affair—a new passion."

"O, no," he replied. "Surely one love can furnish forth a good manny books."

And so we parted almost without meeting. To Galsworthy "democracy" is a mere word, and "the League of Nations" nothing more than an Anglo-American alliance, and Russian Bolshevism, the symptomatic rash of a social disease.

To some of us, on the other hand, the Peace Conference has been a heart-breaking disappointment; democracy has in it the sacred kernel of the brotherhood of man and the Bolshevik republic is the greatest and most unselfish attempt ever made to bring Justice into life.

Galsworthy's Anglicism must not be taken to be the best even in England. He is handicapped by his social advantages. The other day I read a speech of Robert Smillie, the labor leader of the English miners, who has reached a higher height than any of the so-called educated English. At a recent meeting he said:

"The German and Austrian people are not to be blamed for the war. All children are our children, whether they live in England, France or Germany. If it was wrong for the Germans to come over here to kill men, women and little babies with their hellish machines of war, was it not also wrong that we should use the power we have to starve the German women and children?"

The heart of England is not in the educated classes.

But Galsworthy is still growing. His new book "Five

Tales" (Scribner's) forces me to amend the above judgment which I do gladly. As I have said already I am not an admirer of his stories. And at first this book struck me like the rest.

The first story in it called "The First and the Last" seemed to me a failure; none of the personages in it except the lawyer brother was realized at all, and he not realized deeply. Seventy-five pages that you forget at once.

The next story, "A Stoic"—a sort of tale of the city and company promotion and the inherent thefts of the strong man from the weak, is better done; the atmosphere and surroundings are perfectly caught; the ability of the old commercial buccaneer excellently rendered; the man's love of power and riches; his love, too, of a good dinner and a good drink—all splendidly realized; but the whole thing sordid, grimy, not lifted to the sunlight by any passion or any hope. Two hundred pages of stuff for the intelligence; very little for the heart; nothing for the soul.

Almost daunted I began the next story, "The Apple Tree." and very soon I became enchanted; lost in a real love story—a love story most beautifully told. The atmosphere and surroundings perfectly rendered; a great landscape; the English country in spring magically represented:

"Spring was a revelation to him this year. In a kind of intoxication he would watch the pink-white buds of some backward peach tree sprayed up in the sunlight against the deep blue sky, or the trunks and limbs of the few

Scotch firs, tawny in violet light, or again, on the moor, the gale-bent larches in their young green, above the rusty black under-boughs. Or he would lie on the banks, gazing at the clusters of dog-violets, or up in the dead bracken, fingering the pink, transparent buds of the dewberry, while the cuckoos called and yaffles laughed, or a lark, from very high, dripped its beads of song. It was certainly different from any spring he had ever known, for spring was within him, not without."

How fine that is; the lark "dripped its beads of song!"

And the love story itself; the passion of it and the abandonment, more perfectly rendered still. I do not think there are many pages in English of finer quality than this, I am going to quote. The only one I remember is in "Richard Feverel," and this is worthy to be remembered beside that most magnificent love idyll:

"He caught hold of her hands, but she shrank back, till her passionate little face and loose dark hair were caught among the pink clusters of the apple blossom, Ashurst raised one of her imprisoned hands and put his lips to it. He felt how chivalrous he was, and superior to that clod Joe—just brushing that small, rough hand with his mouth! Her shrinking ceased suddenly; she seemed to tremble towards him. A sweet warmth overtook Ashurst from top to toe. This slim maiden, so simple and fine and pretty, was pleased then, at the touch of his lips! And, yielding to a swift impulse, he put his arms round her, pressed her to him, and kissed her forehead. Then he was frightened—she went so pale, closing her eyes, so that the long dark lashes lay on her pale cheeks;

her hands, too, lay inert at her sides. The touch of her breast sent a quiver through him. "Megan!" he sighed out, and let her go. In the utter silence a blackbird shouted. Then the girl seized his hand, put it to her cheek, her heart, her lips, kissed it passionately, and fled away among the mossy trunks of the apple trees, till they hid her from him."

The dreadful tragedy of preferring a commonplace girl to a "lyric love" is brought out, it is true, but not realized so successfully. Megan, the little Welsh girl, who died of love with "beauty printed on her," is simply unforgetable.

Just the last words of the story are shocking. It ought to have ended with Ashurst's repeating his wife's "Something's wanting," by "Yes, something's wanting." But the putting "his lips solemnly to his wife's forehead" should be cut out in another edition. We are not interested in the wife!

There are other stories in the book. I do not remember them. I have read this one half a dozen times already, and it lives with me as part of the furniture of my mind so long as this machine shall last. It is better than "Justice." It is one of the short stories of the world.

Having written this, Galsworthy may do anything, may yet write a masterpiece, will write one, I'd say, were he not an Englishman. In the realm of the spirit that today is a heavy handicap.

Cunninghame Graham
*Drawn by* MOOREPARK

# CUNNINGHAME GRAHAM

CUNNINGHAME GRAHAM, when I first saw him, was something more than a very handsome man: he was picturesque and had an air with him. He might have been the subject of a portrait by Zurbaran of some Spanish noble who had followed Cortès. As soon as I knew him I always called him to myself—El Conquistador. Graham was above middle height, of slight nervous strong figure, very well dressed, the waist even defined, with a touch of exoticism in loose necktie or soft hat; in coloring the reddish brown of a chestnut; the rufous hair very thick and upstanding; the brown beard trimmed to a point and floating moustache; the oval of the face a little long; the nose Greek; large blue eyes that could become inscrutable as agate or ingenuous, responsive; eyes at once keen, observant and reflective; both light and depth in them.

He was never taken for a dandy or merely a handsome gentleman; you felt a certain reserve in him of pride or perhaps of conscious intelligence; he was "some one," as the French say.

I noticed him first at a Socialist meeting. William Morris was there and Bernard Shaw, I think, and Champion, the ex-artillery officer, and Hyndman, the Marxian leader of the party in the mid-eighties. Graham had evidently not studied the economic question; but was enlisted on the side of the poor and the workman, partly by a sense of justice, partly by an aristocratic disdain of riches and the unscrupulous greed that acquires riches.

"Why should we honor the wolves?" was his argument, "who break into the sheepfold and kill, not to satisfy their hunger, even; one could forgive them that; but out of blood-lust. Your rich contractor or banker is a mere blood-sucker; why tolerate him? Pay good watch dogs to protect you and kill the wolves as noxious brutes."

There was disdain of his audience in every word, in his attitude even; he had an artist's contempt for their lack of vision, an adventurer's scorn for their muddy, slow blood.

The next time I met him was riding in Hyde Park. It used to be said that nobody could ride in the Row who wasn't properly dressed, and by "properly" in England they mean conventionally—dark coat, dark trousers tightly strapped over patent boots. But Graham was in breeches and brown boots, as indeed I was; but then he wore a sombrero besides and was mounted on a mustang of many colors, with inordinately long mane and tail.

"Some circus rider," was one remark I heard made about him.

We came together naturally, as outlaws do; for I wanted to know why Graham rode a piebald, and he was eager, as every horse-lover, to extol the qualities of his mount. I found that, like Wilfred Scawen Blunt, the poet, who believed in the pure Arab strain, Graham believed in the speed of South American mustangs. I told him about Blunt and how he had imported some of the best-bred animals from the north of Africa. He had arranged a race with some ordinary English platers, and his Arab fliers had been ignominiously beaten.

Graham wouldn't believe it, and the end of it was we made up a race. We agreed to wait till one o'clock till most of the equestrians had gone home to lunch and then try our mounts up the Ladies' Mile. The horse I was riding was nearly thoroughbred, but only about 15½ hands high, so the match did not look unfair. But the English horse had a rare turn of speed and could do half a mile in about fifty seconds, something like racehorse pace. We told the inspector of police of our intention, and at once, Briton-like, he took a keen interest in the match, and said he would tell his men to keep the course clear.

When we came to Hyde Park Corner about one o'clock we found quite a little crowd; we started at a hand gallop and went down the slope side by side, the crowd cheering "Gryhim, Gryhim! Well done, Gri-im!" in strong Cockney accents. As we breasted the hill I slid forward, crouching on the pad, and gave my horse his head, and at once we left Graham as if he had been standing still. When I drew up at the railings, I was some 200 yards ahead.

"You were right," said Graham courteously: "I'd never have believed it. I'm just as much astonished as you say Blunt was; but you don't ride a bit like a cowboy; where did you get that jockey seat?"

"I'm rather ashamed of it," I replied. "I always rode all the races for our Kansas bunch as a boy on the trail. I was the lightest, and I soon found out that the further forward I got on the withers, the easier it was for my horse. But you ride like a Centaur, with easy swaying balance, like the figures on a Greek frieze. I fall naturally into the professional way of doing everything. I suppose it is my intense combativeness; anyway, I'm a little ashamed of it sometimes."

"Why should you be?" he replied courteously. "I imagine it is the desire in you to excel; and what better desire could a man have?"

"It is the desire to excel," I answered, "carried to such an extent that one is careless of grace or comfort. I sometimes think I should have been better without the American 'speeding-up'."

That race made us friends, for Graham came to lunch with me, and we swapped stories for hours, he telling of the Pampas of the Argentine and Uruguay, giving weird word-pictures of that Spanish and Indian civilization, and I of the trail three thousand miles long that ran from Laramie and the Platte river down through Kansas and Texas to the Rio Grande:

> "The old trail, the wide trail, the trail that the buffalo made."

We had many points of contact; we were both outlaws by nature; both eager to live to the uttermost, preferring life to any transcript of it. Moreover, though he knew Spanish and the religious-romantic Spanish nature far more intimately than I did, and revealed himself in his love of it, yet I too had been attracted by Spain and had learned something of its life and literature, just as he had got to know a good deal about America.

His deep and intimate understanding of the Spanish people had freed him from the narrow English self-appreciation by discovering to him the hard materialism of the Anglo-Saxon nature. Every now and then words fell from him and can be found even in his stories that show this detachment:

"Does any Englishman really respect a woman in his heart?" he asked one day, and I could not but smile, for the same question had come to me so often that I had had to answer it. It is the exceptional man of any race who really esteems the feminine mind and spirit. We reach a certain point in growth where the way is closed to us unless we begin to trust our intuitions and act on them as women do. Then first we begin really to respect women. And as Englishmen like consistency of character and strength better than width of vision and distrust change, without which growth is impossible, comparatively few Englishmen ever reach reverence for what differs from their essentially masculine ideal. Graham felt all this much as I did.

Then, too, he was sceptical of the much-vaunted modern "progress." He saw that the enormous growth of wealth due in the main to man's conquest of nature had increased and not lessened social inequality, and especially the inequality of condition. "The poor today are on the starvation line," he used to cry indignantly, "while the rich are portentously richer than ever before." His sense of justice was shocked and his vein of pessimism deepened by this observation. He did not see that all readjustments take time, centuries even, and, after all, centuries are only moments in the soul's growth. I was attracted by his clearness of vision, and above all by his courageous acceptance of all he did see. Graham had no wish to hoodwink himself, and that was a tie between us.

If he had ever been a student and had submitted to the training of a German university we might have been still more alike; but Graham had always had a silver-gilt spoon in his mouth; he had always had money and position and had learned what he liked and left unlearned what did not appeal to him, and that privileged position has its inevitable drawbacks:

> "Who never ate his bread with tears,
> He knows you not, you heavenly powers."

. . . . . . .

The next time I saw Graham was at a meeting in Trafalgar Square in defense of free speech. I forget what the occasion was; but he was there with John Burns and I think Shaw, and was cheered to the echo. No finer or more characteristic pair than he and Burns could be imagined; his slight figure and handsome face showed the aristocrat at his best, and Burns with his square powerful form and strong leonine head, was the very model of a workingman. Shaw, a sort of Mephisto in appearance, but certainly a man of genius, did not fit in any category. But Graham's gallantry and Burns' resolve and Shaw's talent were all nullified by the brute force of the police. The end of the scrimmage was that Burns, Graham and half a dozen others spent the night in a police cell on some hypocritical charge of obstructing the traffic.

And next morning all the middle-class papers spoke with contempt and disgust of both men, the editors never dreaming that the one was soon to be a Cabinet Minister, while the other belonged to a still higher class.

The next meeting with Graham that made an impression on me was in the House of Commons. In the interval Graham had become a member of the House, and his reception enabled me to judge it from an altogether new angle.

"Every man finds his true level in the House of Commons," is a favorite shibboleth of the English. I had always doubted it and often argued about it with Sir Charles Dilke, who, by virtue of his French training, was peculiarly fairminded.

"The House," I said, "is made up of fourth-form schoolboys with a leaven of men of talent. They want to be fair and are fair to ordinary men; they might even be fair to a man of genius provided he had great parliamentary or oratorical power; but the highest form of genius would have a sorry reception there and a hard time of it."

Dilke would never admit it.

"How do you account for the way they took to Bradlaugh?" he asked.

"After treating him for years like a knave," I replied, "they came to recognize at long last his high courage and noble character, chiefly because he had strong English prejudices, was an individualist and staunch believer in the rights of property; in other words, high character, great fighting power and second-rate intelligence won their hearts in the long run. But the long contest broke Bradlaugh, and he died untimely in the hour of triumph."

"Then what do you say of Tim Healy?" Dilke persisted; "he's clever enough, God knows, and has no English prejudices. How do you account for his success?"

"He's not very successful," I retorted; "even now, after twenty odd years of striving; but take Lord Hugh Cecil; he has everything the English like; great name and place; he stands, too, for all the English household gods; believes in property, in the oligarchy, is unaffectedly religious and goes to church twice every Sunday; and yet because he has a streak of genius in him they won't have him. They give his dull brother, Lord Robert Cecil, place and power; but they keep Lord Hugh at a distance. The English simply hate and fear genius. To them it is an unforgivable sin, and that's why their houses will be left unto them desolate."

Dilke wouldn't have it, yet Cunninghame Graham came to the House and the House wouldn't listen to him; simply gave him, or rather gave themselves, no chance. Of course, he made all sorts of blunders. Every one is listened to in the House of Commons the first time he speaks; a maiden speech takes precedence of all others, and so able men, as a rule, make their maiden effort in some great debate, where they are sure of a large audience. Graham, conscious probably of great powers, wasted this opportunity, and afterwards he would have had to make himself known to the Speaker by constantly speaking to empty benches, and even then would have had to get up half a dozen times on any important occasion before he could "catch the Speaker's eye," as the phrase goes. But whenever he prepared, he tried in vain to catch the Speaker's eye, and when by assiduity he got a chance, the waiting and the rebuffs had taken the steam out of him. And yet he was an admirable speaker at his best, just as he was and is a most excellent writer.

How good a writer he was I learned soon after I took the editorship of *The Saturday Review* in 1894. He came in and told me of a recent visit he had made to Spain and Africa and how he had enjoyed the art of the Prado and the wild, free life in Morocco.

"I've brought you a little sketch of an incident," he said, handing me a manuscript, "if you care to use it."

"Surely," I replied at once; "I'll be delighted; I'm certain I shall have a treat." And so strongly had Graham's personality affected me that I did feel certain he would do noteworthy work.

After he left I found I could not read his handwriting, a dreadful spidery scrawl, so I sent the sketch to the printer and when I read it in print I was charmed. Graham, it was clear, was a born writer of the best; very simple, without a trace of pose or mannerism or effort, getting all his effects by some daring image or splash of color—a strange trait of character or weird peculiarity of mind— and above all by a spiritual sense of the intimate relation between persons and scenes, as if the Gaucho's mind had some of the vagueness and empty void of the Pampas and as if his soul was like that Southern atmosphere, subject to sudden rare storms of singular violence. Graham paints like one of the school of Goya, a Zuloaga, for instance, who has been touched by French influence.

I remember one occasion that proved his genius as a writer triumphantly. One evening I heard that William Morris had died. Next day Arthur Symons asked me to let him write on Morris' poetry; a little later Shaw blew in with the declaration that he wanted to write on Morris as a Socialist.

"All right," I agreed; "but stretch yourself, for Graham will describe the funeral, and his stuff'll be hard to beat."

Shaw grinned; he, too, knew that Graham was a master.

When the articles came in both Shaw's and Symons' were most excellent, but Graham's had abiding value, was indeed literature and not journalism at all. He merely described what had happened; the meeting of a dozen famous men at the train, the dreary walk from the station to the cottage, and then the following the coffin to the grave and the wordless parting. He told how the few flowers wilted and cringed in the bleak wind and how eloquent men were content to exchange glances and hand-clasps and part in silence. Every sentence seemed to drag heavy with grief, and there was a sense of unshed tears and the unspeakable tragedy of death in the very quietude of the undistinguished ending.

A great writer, is Cunninghame Graham! Three or four of his best stories will live with the best of Kipling.

One later impression: I met him at an evening party

in 1912, I think, in the house of a Spaniard named Triano, the Envoy or Ambassador from some Spanish South American State.

I had not seen Graham for perhaps fifteen years; he had altered indefinably. His hair was sprinkled with gray; the slight figure was as well set up and alert as ever; but the fine coloring had faded and the light of the eyes was dimmed; he had grown old, the spring of hope had left him.

The Spanish setting suited him, brought out his dignity and fine courtesy; he spoke Spanish like a native who was also a man of genius, and our host took delight in praising him to me as the only Briton he had ever met who might be mistaken for a Spaniard—un hidalgo—an aristocrat; he hastened to add: He's a great writer, too; isn't he?'

"Yes," I replied, a little hesitatingly, and then the word came to me, the true word, I think, "Graham's an amateur of genius."

"That's it!" cried Triano, delightedly. "I know just what you mean. He does not take his work seriously, doesn't use the file on every phrase, seeking perfection; he's a little heedless and his success haphazardous, eh? His true métier is that of a gentleman-courtier; he should have been English ambassador at the Court of Madrid."

When I talked to Graham that evening I found him saddened. The sense of the transitoriness of life was heavy on him:

"Where are they all?" he asked; "the old reviewers?

McColl, Runciman, Max, Shaw and the rest; do you ever see them?"

"From time to time," I replied. "Shaw is married, you know, and Max, too; Runciman is dead, Wells lives in Essex; and McColl at the Tate Gallery; we are all more settled and none of us getting younger. . . ."

"None of us," he said, sighing; "how fast life streams past! Are you as eager as ever?"

"I think so," I answered. "I look forward as hopefully as I did at sixteen; indeed, I believe I'm more eager, more hopeful, certainly more firmly resolved than I was as a young man."

"I wish I could say as much,' sighed Graham; "life's worth while, of course; but it hasn't the glamor and magic it used to have, and the younger generation aren't very interesting, are they?"

"Some of them interest me hugely," I said; "there's Middleton Murry, with the *Rhythm* he edits, and a young sculptor, Gaudier-Brzeska, and Augustus John and Ferguson and Jimmy Pryde and Lovat Fraser—all gifted, all likely to do big things. . . ."

"I don't know any of them," he said; "where are they to be found? How young you keep!" and then, "Where are you living now?"

Somehow or other this meeting and Graham's sadness made me ask a friend of his a day or two later how Graham lived: whether he was hard up?

"Hard up?" exclaimed our friend; "he has ten thousand a year at least; but he's a Scot and thrifty; 'near,' we call it."

The incident showed me how little I knew of Graham; how reticent he was or proud with that curious secretive pride which is so Scotch and so Spanish.

Graham's stories are almost unknown in these United States, and yet I fancy they would be popular or at least keenly appreciated by the few who know how to read; for good readers are almost as scarce as good writers.

Here, for example, is a picture taken from La Pampa, a story in a book entitled "Charity," that he gave me in 1912:

"Grave and bearded men reined in their horses, their ponchos suddenly clinging to their sides, just as a boat's sail clings around the mast when it has lost the wind."

Or take this portrait of Si Taher, an Arab mystic, half fanatic, half madman:

"Brown and hard-looking, as if cut out of walnut wood; with a beard so thick it loked more like a setting than a beard, though it was flecked with grey. . . His thin and muscular body, which his *haik* veiled, but did not hide, showed glimpses of his legs and arms, hairy as the limbs of an orang-outang. His feet were shod with sandals of undressed camel's skin. His strong and knotted hands looked like the roots of an old oak, left bare above the ground, both in their size and make. He always carried in his hand a staff of argan wood, which use and perspiration had polished like a bone."

Or, in the same book, his picture of his "Aunt Eleanor," almost unquotable, for every line of the ten pages has a new touch that adds to the versimilitude of the portrait. Take these paragraphs:

"Tall, thin and willowy, and with a skin like parchment, which gave her face, when worked upon by a slight rictus in the nose she suffered from, a look as of a horse about to kick; she had an air, when you first saw her, almost disquieting, it was so different from anything or anybody that you had ever met. She never seemed to age. . . . Perhaps it was her glossy dark-brown hair, which, parted in the middle and kept in place by a thin band of velvet, never was tinged with grey, not even in extreme old age, that made her very young.

"Her uniform, for so I styled it, it was so steadfast, was, in the winter, a black silk, sprigged, as she would have said herself, with little trees, and in the summer, on fine days, a lilac poplin, which she called 'laylock', surmounted by a Rampore Chudda immaculately white. . ."

In the same quiet way he tells how the old lady loved horses and rode to hounds, even in extreme old age, and then finally of her death after she had made all arrangements for her funeral and given all the necessary orders, and this by way of epitaph:

"My aunt rests quietly under some elm trees in Old Milverton churchyard.

"Many old Scottish ladies lie round about the grave where my aunt sleeps under a granite slab, now stained a little with the weather, imparting to the churchyard a familiar air, as of the tea-parties that she once used to give, when they all sat together, just as they now lie closely in the ground, to keep each other warm. The rooks caw overhead, and when the hounds pass on a bright November morning I hope she hears them, for heaven would be to her but a dull dwelling-place if it contained no horses and no hounds."

In all these stories the painter's eye and a superb painter's talent. Graham has also done one or two sketches of Paris life, notably "Un Monsieur," which de Maupassant would gladly have signed; but in spite of their mastery, his best work is found in pictures of Spanish South America or of Scotland, the land of his heart and home.

Graham's latest collection of tales, entitled "Brought Forward," just published by Stokes & Company, of New York, at one dollar and thirty-five cents, does not contain any of his best work.

Graham himself appears to have felt this, for he writes a "Preface" to this book, in which he takes leave of his readers and bids them forever farewell.

"Hold it not up to me for egotism, O gentle reader, for I would have you know that hardly any of the horses that I rode had shoes on them, and thus the tracks are faint. Vale."

Eight or nine small volumes hold the entire legacy; in half a dozen short stories you have the soul and quintessence of the gallant gentleman who in life was Cunninghame Graham. The tracks he left are faint, he tells you; the record of his sixty or seventy years could all go in one little booklet; but the final account is not to be made up in this way.

He was born to wealth and place, dowered with perfect health and great personal charm; tempted as only such a man is, he might have been forgiven if he had chosen the primrose way and lazied through life relishing all the flowers and tasting all the sweets. Instead of that, he left his caste and spoke and wrote and worked for the poor and the outcast and the dispossessed. He braved the scorn and hatred of men when he might easily have enjoyed their applause and honor. He faced blows and indignities and imprisonment when he could have reckoned on welcome as a distinguished guest in Courts and Throne-rooms; by choice he took the martyr's way and gave the best of his life to the meanest of his fellows.

And I hold Graham the higher because he made the supreme sacrifice, not in rags and dirt, as the saints selected, still less as one seeking insults and scars, but as a courtly gentleman making light of his good deeds and mocking overwrought pretensions, passing through life with a gay smile and reckless gesture as if it were proper for a man to live for others and to die for them, if need be, and for Justice without the faintest hope of reward.

And so I echo my friend's "Farewell," even though I hope to see him again, for his gallant bearing and courage and talent formed part of the pageantry and splendor of life to all of us, and the ease of his accomplishment as an artist more than atoned for the little carelessnesses in craft of this amateur of genius who was at the same time a most delightful friend and absolutely faithful to his high calling.

Gilbert K. Chesterton

# GILBERT K CHESTERTON

NATIONAL ideals are persistent and recurrent. National poets stand out as landmarks; Schiller in Germany, Victor Hugo in France correspond to Milton in England.

These national idols find difficulty in passing the frontier; Schiller to us is hardly more than a rhetorician in rhyme, and the poses and pretenses of Hugo, his innate theatricality, in fact, robs him of our reverence, while Milton's narrow religiosity, his shallowness of mind, and his incurable hypocrisy as shown in his writings on divorce, hide from us the poetic genius of the author of *Lycidas*.

It is admitted today that Montaigne, Renan, Anatole France are typical and characteristic French writers as Dr. Johnson is perhaps the most typical Englishman of letters.

Every nation sees the neighboring nation's idol as a ridiculous figure. We all remember how Taine found it impossible to discover any greatness in Dr. Johnson; he recognized that the doctor was looked up to by Sir Joshua Reynolds and by Burke, was the literary arbiter of his time in London, yet he can see little or no talent in him, to say nothing of genius. Rasselas is tedious, he says, almost stupid. Johnson's criticisms of poetry almost silly; even his table talk as recorded by Boswell is devoid of high lights. He was a mass of popular prejudices, believed that the American colonists should be "whipped" into submission, and that a woman should accept the faithlessness of her husband meekly; was as superstitious as any old woman, drank tea to excess and made platitudes worse than boring by pomposity.

We all feel that this is a French judgment and omits essentials; we think of Johnson's manly letter to Lord Chesterfield, of his noble endurance of poverty, of his reverence, and above all of his sound masculine understanding and hatred of shams and snobberies, and his occasional gleams of real insight; "the devil, sir, was the first Whig. . . . I can furnish you with reasons, but not with a mind to understand them" and so forth.

We have all a soft spot in our hearts for the great doctor; we understand his whimsies and idiosyncrasies and don't dislike them; a characteristic Englishman, we say, with certain conspicuous gifts.

Gilbert Keith Chesterton was received in London just as if he had been Dr. Johnson come to life once more. Born in 1874, he had already made name and reputation as a journalist by the beginning of the new century. His book on Browning in 1904 and on Dickens in 1906 showed a certain range of interest, while his volume on Shaw in 1909 gave him position. But in my opinion his two self-revealing books are *The Man Who Was Thursday,* which dates from 1908, and the play, *Magic,* written in 1913.

Every journalist and writer in London from 1900 to 1910 knew the Chesterton brothers; the younger, Cecil, was a small replica of Gilbert Keith, and some four years younger.  He was a short, stout man, with round head and round red cheeks, a contradictious temperament and an extraordinary belief in his own ability.  He worked for me on *Vanity Fair* for some months, and told me many stories of his brother and their early life together.  They hardly ever met, it appeared, without disputing, and as they always met at meal time, lunch and dinner were the scenes of prolonged and passsionate controversy.  The were both intensely interested in the happenings of the day and they argued about them unceasingly.

"What was the difference between you?" I asked.

"Gilbert loved to play with words," was the reply, "whereas I took words to mean something."

I cannot help thinking that in *The Man Who Was Thursday,* Gilbert records some of these disputations:

"He came of a family of cranks, in which all the oldest people had all the newest notions. . . His father cultivated art and self-realization; his mother went in for simplicity and hygiene.  Hence the child, during his tenderer years, was wholly unacquainted with any drink between the extremes of absinthe and cocoa, of both of which he had a healthy dislike.  The more his mother preached a more than Puritan abstinence, the more did his father expand into a more than pagan latitude; and by the time the former had come to enforcing vegetarianism, the latter had pretty well reached the point of defending cannibalism."

The first time I met Gilbert Chesterton he made an extraordinary impression on me, as I imagine he must do on most men.  He is not only inordinately fat, but tall and broad to boot; a mountain of a man.  He must have described himself in *The Man Who Was Thursday.*

"His vastness did not lie only in the fact that he was abnormally tall and quite incredibly fat.  This man was planned enormously in his original proportions, like a statue carved deliberately as colossal.  His head, crowned with white hair, as seen from behind, looked bigger than a head ought to be.  The ears that stood out from it looked larger than human ears.  He was enlarged terribly as to scale; and this sense of size was so staggering, that when Syme saw him all the other figures seemed quite suddenly to dwindle and become dwarfish."

I soon found that wine and companionship had the effect of endowing him with an astonishing verbal inspiration; as the wine sank in the bottle his spirits rose unnaturally and the energy of his language increased till his talk became a torrent of nonsense.

I have never met any one in my life who was such an improvisatore in words, who became intoxicated to the same extent with his own verbal ingenuity.  And just as the mist of water overhanging the thunderous falls of Niagara is now and then pierced by some shaft of sunshine, so the mist and spray and thunder of Chesterton's verbal outpouring is now and again illumined by some shaft of wit.  For instance, *The Man Who Was Thursday* won a companion, and here is the comment, merely verbal, if you will, but excellent:

"It may be conceded to the mathematicians that four is twice two. *But two is not twice one; two is two thousand times one.* That is why, in spite of a hundred disadvantages, the world will always return to monagamy." (The italics are mine.)

And that is why, too, the martyrs and guides of humanity are able to survive and do their high work in spite of the general hatred, loathing and contempt; there is always some *one* person who understands and encourages and one is a host in himself.

A side of Chesterton, so to speak, or rather some surface characteristics of him, are splendidly rendered in this book; the heart of him, however, is to be looked for in the noble play, "Magic." I can praise this drama wholeheartedly, because I had again and again coquetted with the idea of writing a tragedy on this same theme.

I never took up the matter seriously because all the symbols of the mystery are so hackneyed and idiotic; but Chesterton used the chairs that move and the table that tilts and the lights that burn with different colors, and somehow or other the incommunicable is suggested to us and we thrill with the magic of the ineffable; he manifestly rejoices in the fact that there is no ultimate horizon; but visions from the verge that set the unconquerable spirit of man flaming. He at least is a believer, a devout believer, in the Christian faith and Christian dogma. It astonished Carlyle that a man of Dr. Johnson's power of mind and thought in the middle of the sceptical eighteenth century should have been able to worship Sunday after Sunday in the Church of St. Clement Danes. But what would he have said of Chesterton, who, after the theory of evolution has been accepted and Christianity has been studied historically for half a century and is now universally regarded as nothing more than a moment, a flower, if you will, in the growth of the spirit of man, can still go on his knees daily in adoration and still believe like a child in a life to come and a Paradise for the true believer! In France, or, indeed, anywhere in Continental Europe save Russia, such a phenomenon would be derided; a man of latters who proclaimed himself a sincere Christian would be regarded as negligible, an instance of arrested development. England, however, is still profoundly religious and Chesterton's passionate affirmations have won him hosts of friends. And when he preaches beef and beer as well and asserts that a man's creed is sacred and his house is his castle and Socialism a dream of the unwashed, thousands more join in applauding the "true blue" Englishman, though he happens to be cursed with a rare talent for words and *will* write instead of making a fortune in some legitimate way. As a matter of course Chesterton became popular in England as soon as he revealed himself; but general adulation and personal popularity do not seem to have injured him in any way; the knots so to speak, in his timber cannot be increased in size or number and so he bears success better than most men.

But what hope is there for him? Or rather, what hope is there for us of getting something better from him than he has yet given. We must fetch around, so to speak, and look at him from another point of view before deciding.

His brother Cecil began better than Gilbert in some respects; he was a convinced Socialist even after he left the Fabian Society, started the "New Witness" and began to harry the millionaire profiteer. At any rate spiritual development was a possibility in his case, a probability even, till he immersed himself in the fighting and died with the colors in France.

Gilbert at once took over the conduct of the weekly newspaper; but he is not so good a journalist as his brother, probably because he is a bigger man and a more original mind.

There is no use disguising the fact; there is a blind spot in me; as a student I could not admire Aristophanes; I could see, of course, that he was magnificently equipped with a talent not only for words but for rhythmic speech superior to any of the Greek dramatists or poets except Sophocles and an absolutely unique gift to boot of spiritual humor and satiric denigration; his picture of Socrates swinging about in the air (aerbaton) and talking paradoxes is delicious und unforgetable, yet, in essentials, Aristophanes was an ordinary Athenian citizen; he had no quarrel with the popular idols; the gods of the Agora called out his reverence and the religion of his fathers was good enough for him. He had none of the insight, none of the aloofness, none of the Sacred Fire of the true teacher. He knew nothing of the dreadful isolation and heart-devouring doubts and misery of the pioneer and pathfinder resolved to widen the horizon and carry the light out into the all-surrounding Darkness. He was never a spiritual guide or leader and his superb talent for speech and controversy only exasperated me against him; such a splendid soldier I said to myself without a cause, always fighting as a mercenary against the Light and the Torchbearers.

In this category of voices without high though, singers without a soul, I cannot help putting Gilbert Chesterton; nothing that he has written or is likely to write is calculated to interest me profoundly; his top-note is "Magic" which is hardly more than a disdainful doubt of the prevailing incredulity. I could admire Coventry Patmore and listen for hours entranced to his praise of the Fathers of the Church; even his mystical faith in the ultimate union of the soul with God in an ecstasy of joy won my sympathy and reverence for it came from the depths of his spirit and was indeed the sap of his most sacred song and psalm; but I miss this impassioned fervor in Chesterton and find him as I find Maurice Hewlett a talent divorced from life, a gift unused, wasted in fact or worse than wasted. A sort of Dr. Johnson, not a heroic bringer of the light, as Carlyle phrased it, not even a heroic seeker after it; but one contented with the wax-candles of the past and resolved to maintain that the tallow drippings are an added ornament to cope or chasuble.

Of course, this is unjust and beside the point. We must thank Chesterton for what he is and what he has given, and not blame him for what he is not. I have read verses of his on "Christmas" that have the touch of high poetry in them; humorous verses, too, that come from the dancing heart of mirth; even his journalism is rayed with thought as in the instance I give above when he says that *two is not twice one, two is two thousand times one;* but there it is, the blind spot in me; the earnestness of the fanatic who cannot accept the terrible fact that "there's nothing serious in mortality," and will condemn another by his own limitations.

Yet I see and know that Gilbert Chesterton is a true man, an original thinker, also, a force therefore of incalenlable effect.

Arthur Symons

## ARTHUR SYMONS

*True love in this differs from gold or clay—*
*That to divide is not to take away.*—Shelley.

One day I was praising an article of Symon's when a London literary man of the previous generation, lifting his brows, said disdainfully:

"O yes; Arty can write. A pity he has never anything to say."

There was just enough truth in the ill-natured jibe to barb the shaft and make it stick in memory: "What has Symons ever said?"

No great story, no extraordinary book, no unforgetable lyric to his credit. Clearly he was not one of the Immortals. And yet what charming things he had written; what an astonishing mastery he had of prose and poetry; how many-sided he was! how well-read, how sincere, how sympathetic! What prevented him from winning a prize where even George Moore gets an "honorable mention?"

I pick up this new book of his, "Cities and Sea Coasts and Islands," just published by Brentano, and find as a frontispiece a late portrait of Symons by Augustus John. John is one of the most gifted painters of the age—a man with the seeing eyes of Rembrandt. He does not possess the Dutchman's generous rich palette, but he is a better draughtsman. And he has painted Symons with the relentless truth we all desire in a portrait; the sparse gray hair, the high, bony forehead, the sharp ridge of Roman nose, the fleshless cheeks; the triangular wedge of thin face shock one like the stringy turkey neck and the dreadful, claw-like fingers of the outstretched hand. A

ARTHUR SYMONS

terrible face—ravaged like a battlefield; the eyes dark pools, mysterious, enigmatic; the lid hangs across the left eyeball like a broken curtain.

I see the likeness and yet, staring at this picture, I can hardly recall my friend of twenty-eight years ago. Symons was then a young man of twenty-six or seven, some five feet nine or so in height, straight and slight, with rosy cheeks, thick, light-brown hair and good, bold features. When he uncovered, the breadth of forehead struck one; but even then the chief impression was one of health—delicate health.

At our first meeting he professed himself an admirer of the music halls, then just beginning to be popular in London; declared with an air of finality that dancing was the highest of all the arts, that it alone could convey passionate desire in every phase from coquetry to abandonment, and that was the deepest impulse of the human heart.

"What are we?" he cried, "but seekers after love? That is our quest from the cradle to the grave. Love is our Divinity, Love our Holy Grail."

He was a Welsh Celt in outspokenness, enthusiastic as became his youth. And at once we went at it hammer and tongs. I would have it that poetry—dramatic poetry—was the most complex, and therefore the highest, of all the arts, and cast scorn on his acrobatics and pirouetting-women with overdeveloped leg muscles and breathless thin smiles!

In the middle of the animated discussion I reminded him that Plato had called music the divinest of the arts, and forthwith, to my astonishment, Symons changed front in a jiffy and took up this new position.

"True! true!" he exclaimed. "Plato was right; music is the voice of sorrow, and sorrow is deeper than joy. Music alone can render the sobs and cries and wailing of the world's sadness. Sadness is deeper than desire, sorrow more enduring than joy; death is the rule, life the exception."

I could not help mocking his transcendentalism. "Hurrah for the exception!" And yet his enthusiasm, his ingenuousness, his love of sweeping generalizations —his brilliant youth, in fact, moved me very pleasantly, attracting me.

Shortly afterwards I received a critical article from him, and was astonished and delighted by his mastery of prose. It was lucid—limpid, even—and insinuating as water, taking color, too, from every feeling and rhythm from its own motion. Praising it one day to a friend, I discovered its shortcomings. "It is French prose," I cried, "not English; it has all the virtues, but it is not sober enough: too agile, quick, following too closely the changes, right-about-turns and springs of thought itself. We English have a stiffer backbone and want something more solid, virile, moderate." It is only fair to add that since those days Symons' prose has shed its Gallic flavor and inconsecutiveness, and is now excellent in every respect. But at that time his prose taught me that he must know French exceedingly well, for every sentence could be turned into French almost without change. The next time we met I remarked on this to him, and he admitted the accomplishment as if it were without importance, as in truth it was. And yet this adaptability is characteristic. Strong, original minds do not possess this chameleon faculty of taking color from the surrounding air.

One day he came to lunch with me, and John Gray

was there. They began talking poetry. Gray's slim book had just come out in its green and silver cover, and he had dedicated a poem to me. Symons declared that he looked upon me as a realist, a writer of stories. "Prose, prose, is your medium," he wound up. "You hammer out figures in bronze." He betrayed his French proclivities at every point. He wanted to be epigrammatic, whereas an Anglo-Saxon would hesitate to sum up a personality in a phrase. A verse of Gray's came up—
The subtle torso's hesitating line
Symons repeated it again and again, delighting in that "subtle" in it and the undulating rhythm, and in return Gray quoted a poem of Symons, and at once it struck me that here was Symons' true field: he would win as a poet or not at all. For there was something light about him, academic—about the pair of them, indeed. They had never been out in the naked struggle of life, I said to myself; cultivated creatures both—flowers of a garden, hedged off from the storms and tempests of the world.

Was it his "Amoris Victima" or a talk we had that made me see Symons as one of the band of "very gentle, perfect lovers" who find the same golden gate into life and into heaven? As soon as you came to know him he made no bones of avowing his Celt-like cult of love, Venus Callipyge, the queen of his idolatry. His frankness was most refreshing to one choking in English conventions.

"Have you ever read 'Casanova'?" he asked me one day as we were crossing Grosvenor Square, in a curious, challenging way, born, I guessed, of a remnant of shyness with an older man.

"I should hope so," I replied. "A most interesting book and a great man."

"I'm delighted to hear you say that," he went on. "Most Englishmen look at him askance, and you're the first I ever heard call him 'great.'"

"There is a volume of his 'Memoirs' always at my bedside," I replied, "and his meeting with Frederick the Great stamps him. They talked on an equal footing. I think I've learned more history from Casanova than from any one. His gamblings and swindlings, love affairs and journeyings paint that eighteenth century as no one else has painted it. He's not only a great lover, but a great adventurer. I profess myself an ardent admirer of Signor de Seingalt."

"And I too," he cried. "I intend one of these days to find that last volume of his they're always talking of. What a thing it would be to get out a really complete edition of his 'Life'! We all want the last chapters."

"Go to it," I exclaimed. "I wish you all success, though I much fear Casanova's end will be dreadfully unhappy. Those who live for the sensuous thrill are apt to have a bad time of it when the senses decay."

"I don't know about that," countered Symons. "Casanova had always thoughts to console him, and I suspect he was a good poet as well as a good Latinist. Perhaps I'll find some of his verses. What fun!"

"All luck," I encouraged. "I always see him in Venice, hastening in a gondola to that convent on the island where he met M., his bright, brown eyes straining through the darkness to the beloved."

"His book ends," said Symons, "in 1774, and he lived till 1798. How wonderful it would be if I could find the concluding volumes! He told the truth about life more nakedly even than Rousseau."

"All the world knows how Symons has since discovered the two missing chapters of the last volume, and, better still, the letters of Henriette, who loved Casanova for over fifty years. Now we are counting on Herr Brockhaus' promise to include all this new matter in a complete edition, which I hope to read one of these days.

It was in 1901, I think, that Symons brought out his first volume of poetry. It was a surprise to most of his friends and to some few a disappointment though the technical skill displayed is extraordinary.

There are light verses of Symons as perfect as the best of Dobson, and some of his lyrics will always be familiar to lovers of good poetry. But, curiously enough, it is in his translations that he reigns almost without a peer. There are some in this book from Santa Teresa and Campoamor which are as perfect as can be, and, like home flowers seen in a foreign land, charm one with the surprise of well-loved beauty. Here are two giving the soul of Santa Teresa:

"O soul, what, then, desirest thou?
—Lord, I would see thee, who thus choose thee,
What fears can yet assail thee now?
—All that I fear is but to lose thee.

> Love's whole possession I entreat,
> Lord, make my soul thine own abode,
> And I will build a nest so sweet
> It may not be too poor for God."

And here is a couplet from Campoamor that might be used as a model by translators:

> "Al mover tu abanico con gracejo,
> Quitas el polvo al corazon mas viejo."
> "You wave your fan with such a graceful art."
> You brush the dust off from the oldest heart."

But I remember some translations in a book published by John Lane which were even finer, I fancy—a translation of the passion of San Juan de la Cruz side by side with a rendering of Gautier's "Coquetterie Posthume," as good as the original. There was even a translation of Heine which forced me to admit that Heine could be transferred into another tongue without loss, a miracle I would never have believed had I not seen it done by Symons and by Thomson. Here are two verses, just to show Symon's astounding mastery:

> "I lived alone with my mother
> At Köln, in the city afar—
> The city where many hundreds
> Of chapels and churches are.
>
> . . . . . . . .
>
> Heal thou my heart of its sorrow,
> And ever its song shall be,
> Early and late unceasing·
> 'Praise Mary, be to thee!"

## ARTHUR SYMONS

There are in this book, too, some lyrics of Symons'—transcripts of slight remote moods that please me intimately; one so musical that its cadence affects me like a phrase of Chopin:

> "Night, and the down by the sea,
> And the veil of rain on the down;
> And she came through the mist and the rain to me
> From the safe, warm lights of the town."

This book, too, contains songs of passion that give us Symons' true measure. Here is his confession:

> "There is a woman whom I love and hate:
> There is no other woman in the world:
> Not in her life shall I have any peace.
> There is a woman whom I love and hate:
> I have not praised her: she is beautiful:
> Others have praised her: she has seen my heart:
> She looked, and laughed, and looked, and went away.

I don't know why, but this reminds me in places of Swinburne's "Leper."

And here is great blank verse—verse that Keats might have signed:

> "The sorrowful, who have loved, I pity not;
> But those, not having loved, who do rejoice
> To have escaped the cruelty of love,
> I pity as I pity the unborn."

And here verse with the organ-tones of Milton:
> "And something, in the old and little voice,

Calls from so farther off than far away,
I tremble, hearing it, lest it draw me forth,
This flickering self, desiring to be gone
Into the boundless and abrupt abyss
Whereat begins infinity; and there
This flickering self wander eternally
Among the soulless, uncreated winds
Which storm against the barriers of the world."

It reminds me of Milton's verse: "In the vague womb of uncreated Night," till the last line, which is Matthew
 I turn willingly to pure Symons—a love snatch:
Arnold:—"And naked shingles of the world"—all reminiscent, I'm afraid; but lovely nevertheless.

"O unforgotten! you will come to seem,
As pictures do, remembered, some old dream.
And I shall think of you as something strange
And beautiful and full of helpless change,
Which I beheld and carried in my heart;
But you, I loved, will have become a part
Of the eternal mystery, and love
Like a dim pain; and I shall bend above
My little fire, and shiver, being cold,
When you are no more young, and I am old."

And here Symons in another mood:

"I have had enough of wisdom, and enough of mirth,
For the way's one and the end's one, and it's soon to the
    ends of the earth;

And it's then good night and to bed, and if heels or heart ache,
Well, it's sound sleep and long sleep, and sleep too deep to wake."

If this too, reminds one of a great poem of Davidson, still no one can deny that the writer of these lyrics has every right to call himself a poet.

And just as Symons has reached excellence as a poet, without, perhaps, winning place among the Immortals, so he has shown himself an excellent critic within similar limits. He is not one of those critics who have remoulded the secular judgments passed on the greatest. He is content to accept the verdicts of the centuries. But he is not afraid, in another book, "Figures of Several Centuries" (published by E. P. Dutton & Co.), to justify his half-hearted praise of Meredith or his overpitched eulogy of Swinburne, and he handles his smaller contemporaries, Hardy, and Pater, the Goncourts, and Huysmans, with intimate sympathy and a fine understanding of their merits and their defects. In fact, as a critic he can stand with Hazlitt, or perhaps with Sainte Beuve, though he is not so methodical and satisfying even as these minor masters. He is more whimsical, more like Lamb, and like Lamb, too often gets to the very heart of his subject through sheer passion of admiration.

And Symons is nearly as good a critic of painting and painters, or, indeed, of music and musicians, as he is of writers. When he calls Zurbaran "a passionate mediocrity," I thrill with pleasure, and he has written more intimately and more convincingly of El Greco than any one else. In fine, a man, take him all in all, of very wide culture and broad sympathies, a rarely good judge of the best in modern literature, a writer in both prose and verse of extraordinary accomplishment.

For fifteen years or so I watched Symons' growth, almost every book showing a distinct advance. One after the other his faults and mannerisms of style disappeared and his speech became simpler, more flexible, dowered with an enchanting wealth of musical cadence and happy epithet.

No such master of prose and poetry has been seen in England since James Thomson, I said to myself; surely one of these days he will write a dozen lyrics of surpassing loveliness. In every respect he is more gifted than Dowson. He is a lover, too, as Dowson was, with Conder's divine sense of beauty; so I waited, eager for the fruiting.

One day I met an English friend in Nice. "Have you heard of poor Symons lately?" he remarked casually. "Is he getting better, I wonder?"

"What do you mean?" I asked, with a dreadful sinking of the heart. "Has he been ill?"

"Then you haven't heard? Oh, it's tragic! He was walking with his wife one day in Genoa, I think it was, when he suddenly lost control of himself and began to break the shop windows, muttering wildly the while, 'Lost! lost!' Lost, indeed, I'm afraid; down and out!"

"Great God!" I cried, "what a pity! what a dreadful loss! What was the cause?"

He shrugged his shoulders. "Who can tell? The last time I saw him, a year or so ago now, he had got very thin. He was always delicate, you know. He looked haggard, I thought, worn, played out, in fact." And his eyes met mine.

I needed no further explanation. Symons had reached the fatal term. About forty a man's powers cease expanding. He needs only about half as much food as he formerly consumed. If he does not draw in and form new habits he'll soon grow unwieldy fat or suffer agonies from indigestion, or both. If he has indulged in youth in any way to the limit, nature now becomes inexorable, presents her bill without more ado, demanding instant payment.

The ordinary man gets over the bad place with a rough jolt or two, but the artist is in dreadful danger, and the lover is almost a doomed man. The Latins called Venus, Diva Mater Cupidinum, and where desire is whipped to frenzy by imagination no strength can withstand the strain. Life to the artist-lover resembles the river above the falls. When he notices that he is in the rapids it is already too late; he cannot stop, but is swept on faster and faster to the inevitable catastrophe. It was a French poet, Mery, who wrote: *"Les femmes ont tué beaucoup d'artistes, mais les artistes n'ont jamais tué des femmes."*

After going over Niagara, Symons struggled slowly back again to life. The terrible experience is written in his haggard mask, in the straggling gray hairs and the withdrawn eyes: *The heart knoweth its own bitterness.*

As soon as I heard that Symons was again in comparative health I could not help wondering about his work. Like the brave soul he is, he has taken the burden of it up again; but I am afraid that the fall was disastrous. He has been in what I have called when writing of de Maupassant, "the most dreadful torture-chamber in life." And I greatly fear that no one who has ever passed more than an hour there will be able to do his best work afterwards.

The experience is soul-shattering.

As the artist's reward is the highest and most desirable in the world, it is, perhaps, only fair that his life's pilgrimage should be the most dangerous. But few understand how desperate is his adventure. Not only must the artist feel more acutely than other men, but he must abandon himself, with every fibre in him, to his sensations and emotions, for he is expected to surpass all previous masters in magical expression of his feelings. And if he thereby endangers health or sanity, who cares? The product is all men ask for. "Paint us the heights and depths of passion as no one else has ever done," is the inexorable mandate.

And his competitors are not merely the men of his own day, but the greatest of all time in a dozen tongues.

And then the critic cavils and compares, awarding three laurel leaves here and five there, and another fool wonders malevolently why the artist doesn't pay his debts, never weighing in the balance the incommensurable debt that the world owes the artist and will never even acknowledge, much less pay. For without the artist the vast majority of men would have no eyes for beauty and scant sympathy for suffering. Their very souls are made for them by the artists whom they despise and maltreat.

But in face of this suffering and this torture of Symons, I want to admit my debt and tell its importance. I have enjoyed golden hours of companionship with him and when "farther off than far away," to use his own phrase, with his books, his moods and lovesongs. There are lines of his, I say, that might have been written by Sophocles; there are some that first came from Milton; others that remind me of "the greatest of all the humorists," as Heine called himself, and there are some of Symons' own worthy to be remembered even among these. Here with the shadows gathering round me, I say *Ave atque vale!*

\* \* \* \* \* \* \*

The Right Hon. Winston Churchill

# WINSTON CHURCHILL

MR. WINSTON CHURCHILL'S life has been a succession of adventures: probably no one living, certainly no living statesman of forty years of age, has seen more of war or of life in its tense, dramatic moments.

As head of the British Admiralty he was the first Cabinet Minister after the war started to be driven from his position by a storm of criticism and contempt; but while other fallen Ministers remained in the limbo of forgotten worthies he alone returned to honor and place as Minister of Munitions and then of War. This singular good fortune deserves closer study.

I had read about him in the newspapers of the day many times before meeting him. When merely a youth he kept himself in the limelight, it was said; but then the limelight in England turned naturally on the eldest son of Lord Randolph Churchill, who had given proof that the genius of the first and great Duke of Marlborough was only dormant. Winston passed from Harrow directly into the army. At school he had cut no particular figure; was, indeed, a very mediocre scholar, knowing even now no French, for instance, though he had three hours a week teaching in it for seven years.

When hardly of age he showed an uncommon thirst for adventure by going off to fight for the Spaniards in Cuba; a couple of years later he served on the North

West Frontier of India. Evidently he was as hungry for adventure as he was careless of learning. A year or so later, he went up the Nile with Kitchener, was present at the battle of Khartum and won unique distinction by condemning his General publicly for desecrating the grave of the Mahdi. His book, "The River War," which had a large sale, showed that he could judge men and events with a certain impartiality as from a height. We were still reading this book on the Nile expedition when he stood for Parliament and the very next year he was in South Africa as war correspondent for *The Morning Post*—evidently a bold, active, venturesome spirit.

During the war with the Boers, only two correspondents came to honor in spite of the rigorous censorship, which made everything but eulogy impossible—A. G. Hales, the Australian, and Winston Churchill. I shall never forget the stir made by one article in which Winston declared that one Boer was worth five or six British soldiers in the field. Like some of us who had already made similar statements in the London press, Winston was at once condemned as an American or worse (his mother was Miss Jenny Jerome, of New York). Telling the truth practically ruined Hales; and if Winston Churchill survived and won through, it was because he was a member of the British governing class by birth and manifestly difficult to suppress.

Winston was captured by the Boers, managed to escape and returned from South Africa to contest Oldham again. This time he got into Parliament and soon began to make a new reputation. He spoke frequently and on many subjects without creating much impression; but he managed to avoid boring the House by pointing his political platitudes now and then with acid criticism of his Conservative leaders. Mr. Ernest Beckett, afterwards Lord Grimthorpe, adopted the same tactics and the pair soon came to be looked on with disfavor by their chiefs. One evening Beckett told me the Conservative Whips had let it be known that none of the malcontents would ever be honored with official position. Mr. Balfour, it appeared, insisted on servility and strictest party discipline.

Finding the way up blocked against him, Winston took the decisive step: he left the Conservative Party in 1906 on the question of Free-Trade, stood for a division of Manchester as a Liberal, and was returned.

In the same year Winston Churchill published a bulky life of his father, Lord Randolph Churchill, in two volumes, which was the occasion of our closer acquaintance.

Ernest Beckett had been a most intimate friend of Lord Randolph Churchill. Indeed, when Lord Randolph died, it was found that he had made Ernest Beckett one of his literary executors, the other being Lord Curzon (not him of Kedleston). It was understood that they were to arrange for the publication of a biography of the deceased statesman. Naturally enough, when they knew Winston wanted to write the life of his father, they gave it to him to do and handed over to him all Lord Randolph's official documents and private papers.

Hearing of me through Beckett,[1] Winston wanted to know me and Beckett brought about a meeting, at lunch in his flat off Piccadilly. At this time Winston Churchill couldn't have been more than thirty-two, yet his hair was already thinning and his figure showed signs of a threatening landslip. To my astonishment he was exceedingly fair (his mother being very dark), rufus-fair, indeed, with whitest skin and the round blue eyes and bulging reflective forehead of his father. He was about five feet ten in height, but much stooped. He spoke with a peculiar lisp, which he afterwards mitigated by lessons in elocution and prodigious practice. He had an abrupt directness of manner and took the lead in all talk as a matter of course. His name and life had evidently given him inordinate self-confidence. He knew me, it appeared, chiefly through the article I had written in the *Saturday Review* on the occasion of his father's death. He was kind enough to call it "the best article which had appeared anywhere"; and added that the Duchess of Marlborough, Randolph's mother, always showed it about as establishing her estimate of her favorite son's genius.

Our talk turned, I remember, on the Boer war: we agreed on a good many points. Whatever he had learned by himself was trustworthy; outside of that he had the ordinary English prejudices. He believed that the Boers, as Rhodes said, had been intriguing to get German assistance because in Kruger's place he would have played

German against Englishman. When I declared that the Boers only wanted to be let alone and disliked the Germans even more than the British and were too conceited to seek help from anyone, he brushed it all aside:

"That would merely prove their stupidity. Of course, they tried to get whatever help they could."

Kruger's trust in God, his belief that standing simply for the right, he would not be deserted in the hour of need, seemed to him ridiculous, incredible.

"Kruger, too, was out for money; all he could get, if half I hear is true."

No argument, no fact even on the other side, could find acceptance or even consideration: his mind was not flexible, his sympathies were narrow; his prejudices invincible.

When we changed the subject he spoke of his "Life" of his father. He wanted to know whether I'd look through the proofs of his book and make suggestions. In a weak moment I consented, fancying that his acknowledgment would do me some good. In the course of the next four months I discovered a thousand new reasons for believing that no son can possibly write a life of his father. Even if he is detached enough to see the truth, he dare not write it, if it is unpleasant or derogatory. Men live in conventions, and, according to the English canon of today, a son must see few, if any, serious shortcomings in his father or he will be regarded as unnatural, —worse than a traitor, indeed. And Winston had no artistic ideal driving him to faithful portraiture.

I was a little surprised to find that he saw all his

father's faults with microscopic enlargement. Randolph Churchill had always had an irritable, imperious temper backed by prodigious conceit. After his downfall these faults were poisoned, so to speak, by an extravagant bitterness.

"You didn't like him?" I asked Winston.

"How could I?" was the reply. "I was ready enough to, as a boy, but he wouldn't let me. He treated me as if I had been a fool; barked at me whenever I questioned him. I owe everything to my mother, to my father nothing."

"Did you never talk politics with him?"

"I tried, but he only looked contempt at me and would not answer."

"But didn't he see you had something in you?" I persisted.

"He thought of no one but himself," was the reply; "no one else seemed to him worth thinking about and as his health grew worse, his selfobsession became maniacal. Towards the end it was pitiful: he suffered dreadfully."

There was evidently no filial piety in this son to cloud clearness of vision.

I soon found that Winston was prudent, too, and seldom acted from impulse. Before every important decision he tried to calculate all the forces and establish the resultant. He had a curiously exact sense of his own position. As soon as he became a Liberal he spared no pains to get immediately re-elected:

"If I don't get in at once, the Liberals may drop me,"

was his fear. "They're under no obligation to find a seat for me. It's at the beginning I may fail."

"Your name would always save you!" I interjected.

"It's not enough. I don't mean to give 'em the chance."

After his election the next question was canvassed even more eagerly, more closely:

"Will Asquith give me office?"

After his first speech in the House as a Liberal:

"Did I do well? Asquith hasn't sent for me? I think he will. Don't you? What do the journalists say?"

How well I remember the interminable talks. I saw him nearly every day, and each morning he would meet me with:

"Nothing, nothing, yet; still I have hopes. So-and-so told me last night that Asquith always took his time"; and so on to: "Shall I get office?"

Or his thoughts would take another turn:

"Suppose he asks me what post I should like; what am I to say? Of course, I'd like to be Financial Secretary of the Treasury; that's the highest place he could offer me, I think; but I couldn't well ask for *that*. It wouldn't look well. I'd hate a minor post on the Board of Trade or somewhere."

"But you could refuse it," I rejoined.

"No, no," he said quickly; "it wouldn't look well; might put his back up against me and I can't afford to do that; can't afford it. I wish I could."

"Why can't you?" I asked again in my ignorance, and got the answer.

"If I once get office I've won. Don't you understand?

I'm not rich; can't afford to fight two or three contested elections; might drop out altogether; but once in office, once a Minister and your Party is bound to find a seat for you. You needn't bother any more. The lists are always open to you and if you can fight, ultimately you'll find your place and your reward."

"Oh, I see," I replied; "of course then you'll take whatever is offered you?"

"That's what makes me so anxious," he replied reflectively. "I must take what's offered; I can't bargain; I daren't."

One morning I found him grave but triumphant; a sort of formal solemnity about his manner.

"Mr. Asquith sent for me," he said. "It's all settled. I'm to have the Colonies. Under Secretary of State for the Colonies." He mouthed the words.

"At last," he beamed; "no more doubt and fighting; no more waiting and longing; Ministerial rank; that can never be taken away. No place I shall ever get will be such a step for me as this—none; not even the Premiership: Asquith was very kind; he has really great qualities."

Not a word about his own fitness; nothing about duty or the work to do. Clearly he was meant to be a British Minister.

"The colonies should give you a chance," I said, "for you have visited a good many of them and can get in touch with the real feeling of those you are supposed to represent."

"Get in touch with nothing," he cried; "with my Chief

and with Asquith. Show him and the other Ministers that I must be reckoned with; the ring is there; now for the fight!"

An *arriviste,* a climber, but not a man of genius, for the great man is always thinking of the work and how it should be done, and not chiefly of the reward.

All this was natural enough but backed, as I have shown in the little discussion about the Boers, by a fixed belief that every one is driven by self-interest and by self-interest alone and that any other motive of human action is negligible.

And the chief interest to him at first was money, he was always more than half American. I sold his "Life of Lord Randolph Churchill" to Macmillans for just double the amount he had hoped to get, $40,000. When I told him the offer had been made and I had accepted it, conditionally, he triumphed.

"That'll make me independent; you've no idea what it means to me; it guarantees success; I'm extremely obliged to you."

And some time later, talking of my idea of selling *Vanity Fair,* he was urgent in the same worldly-wise spirit.

"Get enough to live on, without asking anybody for anything: that's the first condition of success, or indeed, of decent living; that's the prime necessity of life. Every man of us should think of nothing but that till it's achieved. Afterwards one can do what one likes—please keep that in front of you as *the* object of your life!"

His earnestness spoke of intense anxieties in the past and was impressive.

Winston had no other god or goal but success, and the only success he understood was the success of wealth and power and honor—success in the day and hour. His ambition was so intense, his vision of what he wanted so clear, the urge in him so powerful, that I would have forgiven him had he married for wealth and position or at least with an eye to those advantages. It is the more to his honor that he married emphatically for love, a daughter of Lady Blanche Hozier, a girl of extraordinary beauty and charming manners; but with no money and no prospects. The Churchills have since had a son and daughter, and whoever has seen Winston playing with his baby on the floor in his drawing-room will understand that his home-life is a perfect oasis in the desert of strife and labor. His pride in the radiant beauty of his wife is good to see. She is tall, dark as he is fair, and carries herself superbly.

In the year of his marriage, 1908, Winston was made President of the Board of Trade, which office he held till 1910; then he became Home Secretary, and afterwards, to the astonishment of every one, First Lord of the Admiralty. I say to the "astonishment of every one," for the Home Secretary is a far higher and more influential position than First Lord, as it is certainly better paid; but Winston Churchill didn't hesitate to take the lower but more responsible post; for he felt that the war was coming. The event shows that he had divined rightly; he had placed himself in the center of the **stage**, not dreaming that the full limelight would reveal his short-comings as sharply as his qualities. Unluckily for him his blunders were appalling: a few thousand marines sent to Antwerp to hold up 250,000 Germans, and the fiasco of forcing the Dardanelles which, however, was a military and tactical but not a strategical mistake. Winston resigned his post and went to the trenches to fight as a subaltern.

I have now shown, I think, pretty fairly the notable balance which Winston Churchill keeps between sentiment and self-interest. Where feeling should be supreme, as in marriage, he has shown himself superior to sordid impulses; he is not only abler than the ordinary man, he is better, kinder perhaps in equal measure. It now remains for me to frame the portrait, so to speak, by indicating his limitations, which may, however, in turn become qualities or even virtues in his present position.

The desire to grow, apart from success or even away from it, always appeared to Winston Churchill as fantastic or disgracefully affected.

"What good is it to be wiser than your fellow men if they don't or won't see it? What good did it do you to foretell the outcome of the South African War when no one would listen to you or give you credit for it?"

The artist's striving to reveal beauty or to throw a veil of loveliness over what is ugly, or to lift the common thing to significance, left him coldly indifferent.

"I wouldn't waste an hour on making a book of mine better," he would say, "if the extra work would probably pass unnoticed or unappreciated: what would be the good of it?"

And the prophet-impulse, whether of Cassandra-warning or of John the Baptist triumphing, appeared to him to belong to a semi-barbarous or even mythical past. He had scant and merely mouth reverence for writers like Goethe, Schopenhauer and Meredith, who set the course for humanity, and he preferred to be captain rather than himself steer the ship. Ideal aims without reward or visible results are beyond his admiration.

But while this short-sightedness prevents him from being a great man, it will help him to success. It is necessary to aim high in order to go far, but he who shoots straight upwards may be injured by the falling of his own arrow.

Winston Churchill is likely, I'm afraid, to aim too low rather than too high. His contemptuous jeer at the German fleet, "We shall draw them like rats from their hole," was neither wise nor in good taste, was, indeed, a measure of ignorant conceit; but like Lord Curzon's dreadful verses, the gibe must be taken to be popular with the oligarchy and to be, therefore, a part of his bid for leadership. But Churchill does not need to please the aristocratic class; he belongs to it; his weakness is that he does not appeal to the masses so successfully as Lloyd George, for instance, and the working-class in England would rather hear of an advance in the pay of soldiers and sailors or an increase of pension and allowances to the widows and orphans than any insult to the foe.

Winston Churchill is not democratic enough to be popular. He hates socialism without ever having studied it, and if one proved to him that in a perfect state it must have its place just as clearly defined as Individualism, indeed that happiness results from an equipoise between these two opposing forces, he might assent, but it would be a reluctant, grudging admission.

I shall never have done if I go on counting up his intellectual shortcomings. He knows no foreign language; cannot even speak French; has no idea what Germany and her schools stand for in the modern world. He has read scarcely at all, and, outside a smattering of history, is astoundingly ignorant of the best that has been thought and said in the world. However, he knows something about the British Colonies and India from having seen them and in so far can crow over most of his colleagues in the Cabinet.

But he reveals himself even more clearly in his admirations. He loves Gibbon and Macaulay and believes that the stilted, antithetical, pompous English which they affected is a model of good taste. He has no inkling of the fact that simplicity is the hall-mark of greatness in manners as in style. He loves lordly rooms as he loves sounding and ornate words. The only phrase he has invented as yet, betrays his taste: he spoke once of a falsehood as a "terminological inexactitude" and the "mot" had an astonishing success. Finally, Winston Churchill has all an Englishman's disdain for everything that does not harmonize with his ideal; he has no suspicion that there are heights above him as mighty as the depths beneath.

Within his limits, however, he is an excellent servant of the State. He is hard-working to a fault and brave to indiscretion. He was the first Minister to make ascents in airplanes, and as soon as hydroplanes were invented he persisted in going up day after day, in spite of reasonable remonstrance. Once his pilot was killed in an ascent a few hours after he had taken Winston for a flight; but the mishap had no effect on the steeled nerves of the Minister. He went up again next day with another airman as if nothing had happened. Again and again he has been under the sea in submarines; indeed, if personal courage be a high virtue in a statesman, Winston Churchill is rarely equipped.

But what a pity it is that he did not adopt submarines more quickly and develop both them and airships more boldly. Years ago he was challenged in the press to spend millions on submarines and airplanes, but he didn't think the suggestion worth considering. I got the late Admiral Sir Percy Scott to advocate in 1912 a large expenditure on the new weapons, and Scott was one of the few British naval chiefs who had both knowledge and imagination; but the British government preferred to let the French and Germans experiment with the new instruments.

As an administrator Winston Churchill has been cautious to excess and followed his chief war-adviser, Admiral Lord Fisher, very closely. The pair did not blunder to success this time, as British leaders of no higher mental calibre have often blundered before. This war may possibly have taught Englishmen that the time for "bungling through" is over and past. How bitterly Winston Churchill, if he has sufficient imagination, must have regretted the wasted years and unused millions that might have made English submarines and airplanes and hydroplanes the best in the world. There is a Nemesis attending place and power and wealth unwisely used.

I have tried to give a realistic portrait, so to speak, of Winston Churchill, and it appears from it that no great or original stroke of genius need be expected from him in any place. Since he first won office and the consequent pension when out of office, that is, absolute freedom from material cares, he has grown stout and only keeps himself within comparatively decent outlines by strenuous polo. He reads only to prepare his speeches and has no other artistic tastes. But, on the other hand, he is easy of approach and his heart is in his work; he listens to everyone, even though he cannot grasp all that is said to him; in fine, he is an excellent sub'altern: capable, industrious and supremely courageous, but not a pathfinder or great leader of men.

England has always despised genius and stoned the prophets; in her estremity, she had only the capable mediocrities, whom she still delights to honor. She had dozens of Curzons, McKennas and Cecils, any number of Beresfords and Haigs, but no Fulton, no Napoleon, no Paul Jones, no one to play indicating figure and so give value to her millions of recruits; no one to imagine, much less to accomplish, the impossible for her sake, and, for love of her, tear victory from the empty sky and the unsounded sea. Yet thanks to America, she is again victorious and her first use of victory has been to deny freedom to Ireland and to drown in blood the aspirations of India and Egypt to self government and national life.

Alfred Russel Wallace

# RUSSEL WALLACE

THOUGH I knew he was one of the Immortals, Wallace did not impress me at first as a great man. His name, of course, was indissolubly connected with that of Darwin as one who had arrived independently at the idea of natural selection as the cause of the origin of species, and the names of Darwin and Wallace will shine as twin-stars in the firmament of science like the names of Newton and Leibnitz.

More even than this might be said truthfully, for both Wallace and Darwin showed not only fairness but generosity to each other. In 1858 Wallace sent his famous letter on Natural Selection to Darwin, who had written a monograph on the subject in 1842 which had been shown only to Sir Joseph Hooker and Sir Charles Lyell. As soon as Wallace learned this fact he gave all the credit of priority to Darwin, and indeed was the first to christen the new theory "Darwinism." And Darwin, not to be outdone, chided Wallace for speaking "of the theory as mine; it is just as much yours as mine."

Those who realize how jealous even great men are prone to be in anything that touches honor and reputation, will readily admit that this is perhaps the noblest rivalry as yet recorded among men.

In spite of my prepossession, Wallace did not give me at first the sensation of power and originality that Huxley, for instance, did; he seemed a little slow, even in drawing deductions; but patient to a fault, singularly fair-minded and persevering as a natural force. He grew upon you gradually. The more you explored his mentality the wider you found it.

He was interested in every phase of thought; the connection between mathematics and metaphysics, the provoking laws that govern chances and regulate coincidences, the mysterious movements of the human spirit by contradictories, by analogies, by merely verbal dissonance and assonance, the gropings of consciousness in the child, the senile decay of mind and memory, the higher law of sex unions:—he had studied all of them and said something worthful about most of them.

And under the panoply of knowledge his mind moved freely; he questioned this axiom and rejected that much-vaunted conclusion without a shadow of hesitation. Bit by bit he impressed me as some natural force impresses despite its simplicity.

His limitations sound like eulogies; he was so perfectly sane, normal, well-balanced, that he could not even understand the devastating passions of a Heine or a Shakespeare—could not see that such wild excess had any excuse or justification; he regarded the mind as inferior that could not hold all passions in leash without effort. He was not a pilot for stormy seas, but the solid land knew no safer, no more excellent guide. His book on "Social Environment and Moral Progress" is a classic in Sociology as valuable in its way, as his immortal essay on Natural Selection.

His goodness was as memorable as his fairness of vision. He always lived most modestly; never desired riches, never feared poverty, believed implicitly that by devoting himself to his best work, he would always make a decent living.

Though born and bred in England, no snobbism had ever touched him, he felt that the peasant's life, being richer in experience, was more interesting than the lord's. Yet he was of the finest courtesy, kindness and generosity; he loved to relieve any want or alleviate any misery; he said once: "The sole value of riches is the joy of giving."

I knew him for more than quarter of a century and can recall no fault in him—no flaw even. His temper was as patient and quiet and fair as his mind, and his health was almost perfect even in extreme age. In writing thus of him, I feel as if I were ladling out treacle to my readers; but I can't help it; I can't go outside the Truth. Looking back, I'm inclined to think he was the wisest and best man I've ever known. Fortunately this word may be added, I've met dozens of bad men who were incomparably more interesting.

I met Wallace for the first time some forty years ago, just after Henry George's book, "Progress and Poverty," had appeared. Everyone was discussing nationalization of the land, and George's single-tax panacea for social injustice. Englishmen were roughly divided into two camps, those who believed in land nationalization and those who disbelieved in it. Wallace believed in it, yet saw quite plainly that it was only one step in the transformation of the feudal state into an industrial state; but the importance of it as a step forward he preached with astonishing vigor.

I was struck at once by his curious but perfect understanding of the fact that wage-slavery is really more degrading than chattel-slavery; that civilization, or the humanisation of man in society, is absolutely impossible so long as men and women willing to work are under the whip of hunger and scourged by fear of want. He was the first Englishman I met who understood this cardinal fact. He wrote: "Our whole system of society is rotten from top to bottom, and the Social Environment as a whole, in relation to our possibilities and our claims, is the worst that the world has ever seen."

The next time I saw him was in the offices of the *Fortnightly Review*. He and Frederic Chapman, head of the publishing house, had been boys at school together in the west of England; I got them out to dinner, set them reminiscencing, and so by schoolboy memories made Wallace's more intimate acquaintance.

Chapman always asserted that Wallace had changed less than any one; "he is the boy grown large"; but that only shows how little boys and even men know of each other, for the real Wallace was head and shoulders out of poor Chapman's sight.

Later, Wallace used to come to see me whenever he was in London. We often lunched together and spent the evening playing innumerable games of chess; he was not a great player, but a good amateur—careful, not brilliant. Two or three times he stayed with me for a day or two. But as soon as his business in London was finished he hurried "home" to his cottage in the country. Gradually I came to have the most sincere admiration for him as a man of the rarest qualities.

His appearance was prepossessing: he was tall, I should say over six feet in height, and strong though loosely made. A fine face framed in silver hair; the features were regular, well-balanced; the eyes splendid —blue as the sky—the light in them the kindly radiance of genius. Wallace had all the candor of a child, and he met every one with amiability and gentle courtesy. He would discuss any subject with perfect frankness, and would listen to diametrically opposed opinions with a certain sympathy while defending his own views with ability and persistence: his adversary might see some new facet of truth—a very simple and great nature.

It is by the heart we grow, and Wallace kept himself so sincere, so kindly that he grew in wisdom to the very end of his life instead of stopping as most men and women stop growing mentally, almost before their bodily growth is completed. A quarter of a century ago he was quite conscious, to use his own words, that "the materialistic mind of his youth and early manhood was being slowly moulded into a socialistic, spiritualistic and theistic mind." He had crossed that desert of scepticism which I speak of sometimes as stretching in front of the Promised Land. He believed devoutly in God, in a constantly acting spirit of almost unimaginable grandeur and prescience, and towards the end of his life he regarded man as a special creation. His words admit of no doubt. The great apostle of evolutionary science speaks of "the Divine influx, which at some definite epoch in his evolution at once raised man above the rest of the animals, creating as it were a new being with a continuous spiritual existence in a world or worlds where eternal progress was possible for him." The conversion of such a man as Wallace, seems to me, very significant.

Many of his critics have written contemptuously of his latest work, "Man's Place in the Universe," and "The World of Life," but I knew Wallace too well to disdain the gropings or even the visionary hopes of one of the finest spirits that ever wore earth.

I am not inclined to overrate Wallace, though I found myself in agreement with him in this return, so to speak, to faith; for I could never accept what he used to call "the chief article of his creed."

I came late to an appointment one day and found him waiting for me in my smoking-room. His face was transfigured, smiling in a sort of ecstasy. I excused myself to him and said I was sorry to be late.

"It is no matter," he said, "I have been listening to celestial harmonies."

"Really," I exclaimed, "What do you mean?"

"Don't you hear the violin?" he said. "I can hear the music distinctly; one was on my knees playing just as you came in."

I stared at him in amazement; but he was perfectly sincere, yet I could see no trace of a violin.

He held up his hand. "Listen," he said, "the melody is still clear though faint."

I listened, but heard nothing; not a sound.

"You will hear the tunes," he went on, "one of these days, for all who love them, hear them."

"What do you mean exactly?" I asked. "Can you recall melodies with such vividness that you really hear them again, as master-musicians recall music by reading the score?"

"Oh, no, no," he replied quietly; "I am not a musician; indeed until I became a spiritualist I didn't care much about music. I was listening to the music of the spheres, supernal melodies." And his face was like that of an angel; his eyes shining with a sort of unearthly happiness. The transparent sincerity of Wallace had so impressed me that I was more than surprised; a certain awe mingled with my wonder.

I want my readers to understand this man. Fifty years before he had discarded all belief in Christianity; long before most of us, he had applied the doctrine of evolution to religion as boldly as to art or science and had cleared his mind of all childish illusions. But now, in ripest maturity, he came to regard this little Earth of ours as the centre of the Universe and the anthropoid, Man as the Crown of Creation, the masterpiece of Being, an emanation of God Himself with endless possibilities of growth in worlds unrealized.

And this extravagant Gospel was not merely a belief. He had the smiling, unruffled certitude of knowledge. The superstition, as I called it to myself, was baffling.

"Does he believe it?" I sometimes asked myself, as Tertullian said, "because it is incredible?" (credo quia incredible).

Naturally, we had long discussions on these matters. Wallace professed to know that there was a life after death for every man; this life, indeed, he regarded as a mere moment in the existence of the spirit, and wonderful to relate he believed that personal identity would be preserved beyond the grave. I could not follow him in this any more than I could agree with his spiritualism, though I admired the ineffable, haunting beauty of the creed and its incalculable effect upon life and conduct. Still I could not help playing Thomas, and can only affirm that whenever he called up spiritual phenomena before me I was unable to witness the manifestations; with the best will in the world I could never see the violins or hear the celestial choiring. I gave myself to the experiments again and again, but never could catch the faintest glimpse of the undiscovered country that may lie beyond the walls of sense.

Yet who shall say that Wallace was not right? No more simple, sincere and noble soul has lived in these times. My readers may remember how in a previous volume of "Portraits" I have praised Meredith as almost Shakespeare's peer. I can only say here that Wallace has left on me nearly as deep an imprint; he was not so whimsical as Meredith, not by any means so gifted in speech; but more trustworthy in spite of his spiritualism—a fairer and broader, if less gifted mind.

One slightly humorous story may be chronicled here,

for humor is sometimes the natural obverse of intense seriousness.

One evening I found Wallace in a friend's house after dinner. I knew most of the people present; cultured folk of the upper-middle class with a good deal of individuality if not much originality of view. Wallace had been made the centre of the gathering; it was just after the appearance of his book, "The World of Life," which had fluttered the dove-cotes of science by its bold belief in a life after death and indeed in life prolonged in other worlds from everlasting to everlasting. The talk swirled about him in drifts and eddies and he answered every one with extraordinary knowledge and sympathetic courtesy.

At length I brought up the famous prediction of Comte, the great French humanitarian, who asserted that there were two problems that would never be solved by man; one was the origin of life; the other the chemical composition of the stars. Within ten years the chemical composition of the stars had been discovered by Bunsen and his fellow student, Kirchoff, I think, and I related the student legend that has grown up in Heidelberg about the discovery.

The two had been working for a long time on the colors shown by different chemical elements when seen through a prism. They had established the fact that nitrogen, I think it was, left a wavy dark line on a white screen. One day the pair went out to lunch in a hurry, for they had been working late and feared the meal would be over. Bunsen put the prism on the wooden window-frame as he closed the door.

When they returned they saw a wavy dark line on the big white screen.

"Who's been here?" cried Bunsen.

"You must have drawn that line," said the other.

They both stared; suddenly one went over, took up the prism, and the line disappeared. The two gazed at each other while the revelation flooded the mind; the nitrogen line had revealed itself in the rays of the sun! The mystery of mysteries was solved. We can tell the chemical composition of stars that may have vanished from the heavens a thousand years before we were born.

"But will the origin of life be discovered as easily?" I asked to change the subject.

Wallace replied, as I knew he would, that sooner or later man would divine all the secrets of nature, for he held all the keys in his own being. And he went on to say how this problem of the origin of life had teased him once in the far East for six or eight months. He had traced life back to its simplest forms and found it hardly more than a power of motion; as undeveloped in certain marine animals as in certain plants that also can move from place to place.

"If the monies we now spend on armaments," he said, "were spent on the endowment of science for one century, that problem and a thousand others of more importance would certainly be solved.

"Think," he went on," that we do not yet know how

even sex is determined; our ignorance is abysmal, criminal.

"But one day we shall be able to create Frankensteins at will and perhaps endow them with wisdom and goodness as supermen to teach our children."

"Wonderful, wonderful," piped up a little man from the background; "but I think some of us would still prefer the old-fashioned way of creation."

A shout of laughter broke the spell; after that we talked of lighter things. It is only fair to say that Wallace laughed as heartily as any of us. Wallace's understanding of the evils of our present day competitive system and the dangers of the selfish gospel of "Everyone for himself," was almost uncanny. In his last book I find, if not a prediction of the world-war, a premonition of the catastrophe which the national and individual selfishness of our time was fated to produce:

"There are, however, indications that the whole march of progress has been dangerously rapid, and it *might* have been safer if the great increases of knowledge and the vast accumulations of wealth had been spread over two centuries instead of one. In that case our higher nature might have been able to keep pace with the growing evils of superfluous wealth and increasing luxury, and it might have been possible to put a check upon them before they had attained the full power for evil they now possess.

"Nevetheless, the omens for the future are good. The great body of the more intelligent workers are determined to have JUSTICE."

If the English Order of Merit had any meaning Wallace's name would have figured in the list when the Order was first created instead of the names of second-rate generals and admirals whose service to mankind never rose above the quarterdeck or mess-room table.

But Alfred Russel Wallace was too great to be seen or understood by any of the kings or ministers or courtiers; his work and his fame, his noble wisdom and simple life belong to humanity—are indeed as Thucydides said of his great History, part of the possession of men forever. He was too noble even to be mourned at death; the best of him lives on in those he influenced; his memory is an encouragement—his achievement an inspiration.

Thomas Huxley

# THOMAS HUXLEY

NATIONS like individuals have ideals and complacently believe that they are admired by others on account of them. Like individuals, too, nations frequently misssee themselves. For instance, Germans are always vaunting their "Redlichkeit und Treue," though few foreigners would be found to admit that the chief Teutonic virtues were honesty and loyalty rather than industry and ambition.

In the same way the French plume themselves on being chivalrously brave and generous to a fault, whereas they are thrifty to meanness, high spirited rather than chivalrous and possessed of a keen sense of truth and justice.

The English, on the other hand, are convinced that they are a plain, sincere and outspoken folk who love truth and hate a lie; in spite of the fact that they think more of appearances than any other race and have a far keener sense of physical beauty than of truth.

Our ideal as a rule is complementary, made up of what we lack of perfection and no proof of an approximation to it.

Now and than, however, a man appears who represents in himself the ideal of the race, and it is interesting to notice how he stands out from the crowd and is always rather respected than loved. The only Englishman I ever knew who came near realizing the English ideal was Thomas Huxley—a very honest, outspoken plain man who was as devoted to truth as nine-tenths of his countrymen are to social pretences.

I cannot say I knew Huxley intimately, though I met him often enough; he was a whole generation before me, and I have again and again had occasion to notice that one can only know intimately the men of one's own time or by gift of frank sympathy or similarity of striving some few among one's juniors.

Huxley's person was as strongly marked as his mind. He gives his height somewhere as five feet eleven; I should have guessed him about five feet nine or ten, spare in figure with square shoulders, erect carriage, and vigorous, abrupt movements. The photograph I reproduce gives his features, but does not convey the challenge of the quick dark eyes or the pugnacity of the prominent cocked nose, or the determination of the heavy jaw, bushy eyebrows and clamped lips:—a fighter's face, if ever there was one, and the face of a Celt at that; he reminded me always of Slavin, the Irish pugilist, though Slavin did not show so combative an air.

And the mind did not belie the outward. Huxley was as pugnacious as any Irishman, as argumentative as any Scot; but one remarked almost immediately that he took no unfair advantage in controversies, and even in the heat of dispute never indulged in exaggerated statements or misrepresented his opponent's case.

His uncompromising love of truth made him the great naturalist. It was impossible not to realize the high and noble allegiance of the man. He himself bears witness to the general contempt of truth in England, and his loyalty to it in his fragmentary "Autobiography," where he speaks of "that mellifluous eloquence which, in this country, leads far more surely than worth, capacity or honest work, to the highest places in Church and State ... I have been obliged to content myself through life with saying what I mean in the plainest of plain language, than which I suppose, there is no habit more ruinous to a man's prospects of advancement."

In France and Germany such plain speaking rather helps a man; but in England, as in the United States, the moment you dissent from the common opinion, you are tabooed. Paine is still regarded here as anything but a patriot.

I do not know exactly when my personal acquaintance with Huxley began. Shortly after I became editor of the *Fortnightly Review* I wrote to him telling him how much I admired his work and hoping that we might meet, adding that if he had anything to say on matters of thought or morals I should be delighted to publish it.

In reply I got a pleasant letter from him inviting me to call, and shortly afterwards I called.

His perfect sincerity, the entire absence of pose or pretence in him, won me at once, and as both of us loved thought and tongue-fencing we were soon at it hammer and tongs, while strolling up and down his garden. Something he said about morality started me off.

"Curious," I said, "that just when we should be taught morality—at school, when our boyish minds are as plastic as our bodies, we are trained in all sorts of immoralities!"

"Quite true," he exclaimed, "I had not much schooling,

but I agree with you that the school influences were the lowest I have ever known. I have met all manner of men in my time—good and evil—but I never met such an irredeemable set of scoundrels as at school. The boys were bad enough with their bullying and cruelty, but the masters and the atmosphere were as bad as bad could be."

"How do you account for it?" I asked, "that in spite of this, most Englishmen are resolved to praise their schools and school life."

He shrugged his shoulders.

"An extremely puzzling question," he remarked thoughtfully. "I have no solution for it."

"Perhaps," I ventured, "the majority have such low morals that they may profit by what would soil and bruise some of us."

"Possibly," he remarked, evidently refusing to go into the matter.

Another point of agreement between us arose from something I said in one of our first talks about the difficulty of making a decent living in England by literature.

"Still harder to get a living by science," he said, "much harder. There are so few places for men of science, and almost no endowment for scientific research: I should have thought the literary man what with papers and magazines and books could get on much better."

"I was thinking of honorary rewards as well," I interjected, "immediate recognition by one's peers. At twenty-five or twenty-six you were elected a Fellow of the Royal Society; the following year you got a medal;

everyone regarded you as a man of great distinction; you could marry and do as you wished."

"In the honor way,' he replied, "I think you are right; all the bigwigs in science were very kind to me from the beginning, and I believe the bigwigs in literature are not kind to the young men; perhaps because the training in science is training in truth and in appreciation of all good work; but in money rewards I think men of science are probably worse off than men of letters. I had to serve longer than Jacob for my wife; we were engaged eight years ago before I could venture to marry.

"What used to annoy me at first was that first-rate men like Owen, who had a European reputation second only to that of Cuvier, only received $1,500 a year as Hunterian professor, less than the salary of many a bank manager. Forbes, too, and Hooker were first-rate men; had they turned their abilities to business they must have made large fortunes; yet they could scarcely live. Some day or other a business world will find it must pay men of science infinitely better than it does to-day.

"But after all," he went on; "the material rewards do not matter much, so long as one gets a chance to do the best in one, and I cannot say that I should have done much better if I had had heaps of money."

"That is the motive power in us, is it not?" I cried. "To do the best we can—the best in us."

"Surely," he rejoined, "I used to call it my demon which drove me to work and would give me no rest till I had reached the highest in me."

Huxley would not promise to write for me, telling me

he was pledged to Knowles, the editor of the *Nineteenth Century*, a friend of many years' standing.

"You see," he said, "we old fellows like sugar, and Knowles gives me lots of it—a proof of second childhood, I suppose," and he laughed half shamefacedly.

As soon as my first story came out in *The Fortnightly Review* I sent it to him and asked him what he thought of "A Modern Idyll." I quote from his reply:

"Hodeslea, Eastbourne,
"June 2, 1891.

"My dear Mr. Harris:

"I greatly delight in stories, and that which you have been so kind as to send me is of the kind which I specially appreciate, and very rarely have the chance of reading.

"Indeed, except Browning and Daudet, I do not know among the authors with whom I am acquainted, where I should find such a true and subtle psychological study. Alike in conception and execution 'A Modern Idyll' strikes me as a very thorough piece of work—so far as it goes...."

He went on to suggest that I should continue the story, expand it into a long novel; he thought it a "grand subject."

I afterwards sent him "Montes," but he did not care so much for it. I wanted to meet him again, so I called and found him this time not frank and sincere merely, but cordial. He would hardly believe that I had written no stories before; that both of the stories I had sent him were my earliest attempts in fiction. He praised the reticence in the telling, citing Goethe's great word:

# THOMAS HUXLEY

"In der Beschränkung zeigt sich erst der Meister."

I wrote to him a day or two afterwards, telling him how I had been attacked by the Rev. Newman Hall and other clergymen and in the press for my outspokenness in "A Modern Idyll.'" He answered me in this postscript, which I give in facsimile: *"The Public, as Mr. Bumble said of the Law, "is a hass". Write to satisfy yourself. The public may kick up its heels at first; but will surely follow with true asinine docility in time."*

Such frankness, such a modernity of outlook seemed to me extraordinary in an Englishman, and delightful to boot. I was very eager to find out about his youth; had he sowed wild oats? He was just as frank about this.

"I am ashamed of it," he said; "but in my youth I committed all sorts of sins—few worse men; all the rest of my life has been a painful climbing up out of the mire towards better things."

"What helped you most?" I asked.

"Carlyle, I think," he said; "more than any man; he taught me that one can have a deep sense of religion without any Christianity or theology.

"Then there was my work; but most of all love was my teacher—love for my wife showed me the beautiful things in human nature, and then love for the children taught me more from day to day." . . .

I began to think him one of the bravest and wisest of men, especially when I found that he held the sanest view of personal immortality.

"I see no reason for believing it," he said; "on the other hand I have no means of disproving it. I perhaps might say I desire it, but my work has forced me to make my aspirations conform themselves to facts, and not try and make facts fit my aspirations." He paused for a while, and then went on, "the thing that always impresses me most is the absolute justice of the system of things. The gravitation of suffering to sin is as certain as the gravitation of the earth to the sun.'

"Great goodness!" I cried; "you cannot hold that faith; that is what the old Jews seem to have believed in—the ancient Hebrew creed; but Job saw that the belief would not hold water,

"He declared he had been righteous and just all the days of his life and yet was plagued beyond enduring."

"I care nothing about Job," replied Huxley, and his lips tightened and his jaw stuck out. "It is plain to me from my own life and the life of others, that the wicked come to grief and the righteous to happiness and joy."

"Great Scott!" I ejaculated. "Your creed is simply incredible. A drunken father strikes his wife and the child is born a cripple, and in consequence suffers life-long agony. Can you see justice in that? Justice in the crucifixion of Jesus; justice in the poisoning of Socrates; justice in your own small pay and being fenced away from the kingdom of love for eight years. Justice!"

Again his lips tightened.

"Of course," I said; "there is a sort of rough justice in the world—an approximation to justice. We are all conscious of that. Conscious that if we get drunk we shall probably have a headache next morning; but I have sometimes drunk a good deal too much and been benefited by it. It is the perpetual terrible injustice of life that is apalling, that distracts all the sympathetic and sensitive spirits, and leads to soulnumbing despair." He shook his head and changed the subject.

It was that talk which led me to study Huxley. There were dreadful limitations in him. I began to see how English he was—shallow, I mean, not deep-souled. The English are good workmen; they have no great thinkers. Their success in practical life comes from shallowness of feeling; they will never be like the Jews, saviours of men, or like the Greeks and steer humanity to new ideals.

But I felt sure I could trust Huxley's instincts of fair play, and so I went at him again for an article. I wanted him to write on the ethics of evolution, and felt that if I provoked new thoughts in him he would do it for me. He began by saying again:

"I am so bounden to Knowles," adding, with his habitual frankness: "I suppose I shall have to write for you, too.

"The phrase 'the survival of the fittest' is ambigous, as you say. 'Fittest' has a touch of 'best' about it—a sort of moral flavor, whereas in nature what is fittest depends upon conditions.

"If our world were to grow cold the survival of the fittest might bring about in the vegetable kingdom a growth of humbler and humbler organisms till the 'fittest' might mean nothing but a lichen; but in the evolution of man there is an ethical process which has grown out of the cosmic process and limits the area of struggle and competition. We are slowly growing better.

"At first the ape and tiger instincts are pretty dominant, but as soon as families are grouped into clans a blood tie is engendered that assures a certain loose unity, and the spirit of the herd comes in to restrain individual assertion. This sympathy with others of our kin is the germ of ethics, and so we have the evolution of that altruistic feeling which we call conscience."

"I know all that," I said, "but it won't do for me. There are qualities in us which cannot be evolved into higher and richer forms, for they tend to self-destruction. Pity, self-sacrifice, the desire that comes to one sometimes for noble self-immolation. It causes a man who cannot swim to jump overboard to help a drowning person. You cannot tell me that that tends to survival; it leads to his drowning, and so prevents him from transmitting his qualities to his kind. Sympathy is a source of weakness in the struggle of life, and should not go a bit beyond the necessities of the case; but it is not even honored by us till it goes far beyond necessity, far beyond even what we regard as reasonable."

"Yes, that is true," Huxley admitted musingly. "It is difficult to be sure about the matter."

"I remember reading once of an Oxford man," I went on, "a Fellow of his college, who jumped in front of a runaway horse in order to pull a poor old apple woman out of danger. The old woman was saved, but the scholar's thigh was broken and he died a week or two later. I remember Francis Newman, brother of the Cardinal, telling me that he thought the man had acted wrongly—disgracefully—throwing his valuable life away for a worthless one; but I insisted that that was the essence of all self-sacrifice. If it were reasonable we all ought to do it, but our admiration went to the self-sacrifice that was unreasonable."

"I see, I see," cried Huxley; "it is, of course, very difficult to decide. You may be right. I will try to write something for you." And we left it at that.

He was 66—thirty years older than I was—and just as willing to force his mind to occupy itself with the furthest reaches of thought as he could have been as a young man. But I was always conscious of limitation in him. He had not anything like the depth of sympathy or width of mind of a Carlyle, or a Meredith, to say nothing of Goethe or Shakespeare.

We lunched together this same year and talked about politics. We agreed in detesting Gladstone, but though he spoke with some admiration of Parnell he suddenly burst into a tirade against the Irish. Healy and Sexton had promised fidelity to their leader, and now declared that they only did it, believing that Parnell would resign—a sort of letter of commendation to a servant if he took his discharge easily.

"What a pack of liars," cried Huxley. "That is at the bottom of the whole Irish question. The Irish cannot tell the truth."

He made me smile. At bottom he was so very English.

"What are you grinning at?" he barked.

"At you," I replied, "and your sweeping condemnation. I have seen no Englishman yet with the sensitiveness for the truth I have known in several Irishmen. The source of the Irish trouble is the fear on the part of the English that the Irish will outdo them. The reason they got rid of the Parliament in Ireland was because the debates on College Green were so much more interesting than those in Westminster. They would be again to-morrow if we had an Irish Parliament. And the Irish would try all sorts of experiments in economics; they might even nationalize the land; probably would; and the English are frightened of that, too."

Seeing him frown I went on maliciously. "The land

must be nationalized in Ireland because Ireland is like a saucer. You cannot drain your land when your neighbors' water is running into it; the first act of a great Irish republic would be to nationalize the land. They might teach you English all sorts of lessons and you are most unwilling learners."

"That is true," he cried, laughing; "you have got me there."

A little later we had a talk about his contest with Gladstone over the Gadarene swine.

"The idea," I said, "of your arguing with Gladstone about such nonsense! You might just as well go into a ring to wrestle with a naked savage whose body was smeared with oil."

But he would not have it; he had all an Englishman's peculiar reverence for position, "Gladstone was twice Prime Minister . . . enormous influence,' and so forth and so on.

A little later I got an essay from him on that curious moral difficulty I have already spoken of, which the doctrine of "the survival of the fittest" does not elucidate. He met the point frankly; but he would not admit, as Alfred Russel Wallace admitted, that our admiration for self-sacrifice could never have come from the herd-feeling, for it goes beyond reason and is condemned by the herd-feeling. To the English state the life of a gifted young professor was far more valuable than that of an old apple-woman. Our admiration of heroism is as intuitive as our love of beauty; is, indeed, as Wallace saw, the best proof that some divine impulse is working in us and through us to a fulfilment beyond our imagining.

Huxley's mind had its limitations; his sympathies were somewhat narrow; but the beauty and nobility of his character grew upon one. He was generosity itself to all youthful or worthy striving, and bit by bit, the enthusiasm of the younger scientists helping, he came to a position of unique authority. When he was made of the Privy Council everyone was astonished and rejoiced, as one is astonished in England when honor is paid to the honorable.

So, after all his controversies, and they were as many as the years of his life, he came in the fullness of time to leisure and dignity and the enjoyment of the winged hours.

His married life had always been almost ideal; he never sent an article to the printer before his wife had read and declared it good, and whenever she objected to any passage he knew at once that it needed revision.

All his life had been a moral growth, and his greatness of character often brought him to extraordinary wisdom. For instance, he was approached shortly before his death by an anti-militaristic society, and he answered them in the following words, which I think worth weighing and assimilating today, though they were written offhand five and twenty years ago.

"In my opinion it is a delusion to attribute the growth of armaments to the 'exactions of militarism.' The 'exactions of industrialism' generated by international commercial competition, may, I believe, claim a much larger share in promoting that growth. Add to this the French thirst for revenge, the most just determination of the German and Italian peoples to assert their national unity; the Russian Panslavonic fanaticism and desire for free access to the western seas; the Papacy steadily fishing in troubled waters for the means of recovering its lost (I hope for ever lost) temporal possessions and spiritual supremacy; the 'sick man' (Turkey) kept alive only because each of his doctors is afraid of the other becoming his heir."

With Huxley died a great moral influence and no one in the present generation occupies the throne he left vacant. When a generation or more elapses before anyone is found to fill your place, you may be said to have achieved a certain measure of immortality. Huxley was always contemptuous of fame, declaring frequently that he would not give a button for posthumous reputation. Nor has he left any work that will enshrine him in the memory of men. But his life and example were inspiring and he will live on in the spiritual influence he exercised over many of the best men in his own time.

Louis Wilkinson

## LOUIS WILKINSON

BY every right of blood and birth Louis Wilkinson should have been among the most conventional of Englishmen. He was born and brought up in the straitest sect of the Pharisees and yet appears to have sucked in revolt with his mother's milk. I have no ready-made or even reasonable explanation of his phenomenon; Wilkinson must be accepted as a "sport" just like a child of ordinary parents who is endowed with six fingers.

He was born December 17, 1881, at Aldeburgh in Suffolk. His father was the Rev. Walter Wilkinson, Fellow of Worcester College, Oxford, distinguished in the chess world as an amateur. This Walter Wilkinson travelled all over Scandinavia, and "discovered" Ibsen before Mr. William Archer, but failed to interest anyone in the slightest degree in Ibsen's work.

Louis Wilkinson was educated at Radley College, one of the large English "public schools," after having gained a classical scholarship there as a result of the classical education received from his father. In 1899 he won another classical scholarship at Pembroke College, Oxford—an event which had a sequel of some significance. From his first term at Oxford, Wilkinson displayed a most violent antagonism to the ruling undergraduate caste—the "bloods," in 'Varsity parlance; or, to use a term that will convey a clearer description to present-day American readers, the *Junkers,* who based their pretensions to ascendancy in college and university life on their prowess in sport and in athletics.

Wilkinson, and his few friends who sympathized with his rebellion, fought the pretensions of this governing class in every possible way, by propaganda and by direct action. The "Junior Common Room", a club to which access was by right free to every member of Pembroke College, had been for some time closed to all except the Junkers and their friends and toadies. This arbitrary denial by the few of the rights of the many was the object of special attack by Wilkinson and his party. A manifesto was drafted, couched in phrases which no doubt revealed all the pompous gravity of adolescence, protesting against the claims of a handful of men to arrogate to themselves the privileges that belonged to the Commonwealth. A surprisingly large number of signatures was secured, but the manifesto failed, and the college authorities showed unmistakably that their sympathies were with the Junker caste.

Meanwhile, an insolent notice posted by the leader of the athletic party, that "it was not only the duty, but the business," of all the members of the college to run along the towing-path while one of the university rowing races was in progress, further helped in bringing matters to a head. Wilkinson and his friends of course refused to go near the towing-path. Shortly afterward, Wilkinson's rooms in college were raided in his absence by the leaders of the athletic set, and the furniture mauled after the fashion of such "raggings."

A special point was made of the mishandling of a

framed photograph of Oscar Wilde, with whom Wilkinson had corresponded for two or three years before his death. He had never met Wilde, but entertained and expressed high admiration for him as an artist and a revolutionary figure. This fact, and the further fact that Wilkinson made no secret of his contempt for the forced routine of college chapel services, encouraged his more malignant enemies in the hopes that he and his friends might be laid low by the time-honored reactionary trick of accusations of immorality and blasphemy.

Their dangerous activities in opposition to the Junker régime would thus be stopped forever. Painstaking efforts of inquiry failed, however, to collect even the most meagre evidence of immorality against either Wilkinson or those associated with him; consequently this charge was soon abandoned, and the "Junior Common Room" men determined to make things hot for the offenders by a continuation of the policy of "ragging" their rooms rather than by laying "information," which had so obviously little or no relation to truth.

But the Wilkinson faction was not inclined to take this kind of treatment in the proper spirit of humility. Being in a hopeless minority, they realized that resistance of the usual kind was foredoomed to failure, and they therefore, perhaps somewhat in the spirit of melodrama, provided themselves with revolvers, and advertised their determination to use them in the face of any assault either on their persons or their property. The threat was put to the test, and the raiders of the next set of rooms, confronted by loaded firearms, thought better of their intention and retired. No further attempt at violence was made: resort was now had to other means and the cooperation of the college authorities was secured by the undergraduate oligarchy.

The master of Pembroke College was then, and I believe still is, the Right Reverend John Mitchinson, sometime Bishop of Barbadoes. This individual signed his letters during his episcopacy "John Windward Isles," thus courting a deserved ridicule, which annoyed him extremely. He was a didactic disciplinarian of the worst Prussian type, with all the tyrannical impulses which so frequently obsess men of low birth who have risen to authority. He was a religious bigot and a fanatical conservative. Obviously no head of a college could have been better qualified by character and opinions to collaborate with the enemies of the Wilkinson party. How the undergraduate Junkers "worked" him is not clear, for secrecy shrouded their manœuvres, but the task of aligning him against such rebels could not have been difficult.

The undisputed fact is that he summoned Wilkinson and four of Wilkinson's most "dangerous" friends, and summarily informed them that they were no longer members of the college. The reason given was that they had been proved guilty of "blasphemy", but not a single specific charge was put forward, and therefore any defense, even had it been allowed, was out of question. The men were not confronted by their accusers. There was not the remotest semblance of a trial. The Bishop contented himself by saying that the contract between the college and the undergraduates was one terminable at pleasure on either side, and that he chose to terminate it. The real reason, of course, was that Wilkinson and his friends held and acted on opinions that ran counter to the interests of the college oligarchy; therefore it was necessary to get rid of them.

The cup of Wilkinson's guilt ran over, when it was known that he opposed the Boer War and was a contemptuous critic of British jingoism. In 1901 such an attitude ensured a dangerous unpopularity.

Mr. Labouchere's journal, *Truth,* ran a series of articles under the title of "A 'Varsity Star-Chamber," exposing what he called "The Pembroke College Scandal."

In 1902 Wilkinson, helped enormously by the influence and the exertions of his father, who realized at once the grossness of the injusice that had been committed, matriculated at St. John's College, Cambridge. He now turned from classics to the study of history, winning an Historical Exhibition in 1903, and graduating with honors in 1905. In this year he published his first novel, "The Puppet's Dallying," which, though naturally immature, had a certain *succès d'estime,* being favorably noticed by the more important London journals.

In the summer of 1905 Wilkinson was invited by the Philadelphia Society for Extension of University Teaching to come to America for a six months' lecture tour. During the period from September, 1905, to March, 1906, Wilkinson laid the foundation of his prestige as a lecturer on literary and social subjects in this country, and he has lectured over here in the winter months continuously to the present date, with the single exception of the 1914—1915 season, which he spent in Spain and Italy. In 1914 he received the degree of Doctor of Letters from St. John's College, Annapolis, in recognition of the value of his lectures there. In 1909 he had become co-founder with Dr. Arnold Shaw of the University Lecturers' Association of New York, an association that was speedily joined by John Cowper Powys and other distinguished speakers. The friendship between Powys and Wilkinson is a curious example of the attraction of opposites, for Wilkinson's antipathy to the essential elements of Powys' outlook on life and literature is deep-rooted.

From 1905 to 1914 Wilkinson, disgusted by the imperfections of his first novel, made no serious attempts to write, but in the summer of 1914, at Siena, he began his second novel, "The Buffoon." It was completed in the following year, and published by Knopf in the spring of 1916 and in England by Constable's.

During the summer and fall of 1916 Wilkinson wrote his third novel, "A Chaste Man," which was published in the fall of 1917.

The scene of the novel is laid in Chiswick, a suburb of London; the character of the hero is anamalous yet peculiarly English, for in England a Joseph is still possible if not praiseworthy, whereas in every other quarter of the globe a Joseph would be ridiculous and disgraceful, if not utterly inconceivable. The philandering hero who wins the young girl's love and then has scruples about embracing her, does not impress me in spite of his chastity, though he is excellently drawn; his cold snobbish wife, too, fails to reach my sympathy, but the Flynn family—the wise and outspoken but drunken Irish father, the three unconventional vividly differentiated daughters and the boarders—is of most pathetic interest, and the slip of the hero's sister gives the very imprint of life itself, an impression only reached by consummate art.

It is exasperating, though natural enough, that England should still lead these United States in all literary achievements. I have just read half a dozen American novels by well-known writers, but not one of them can be compared either as works of art or as transcripts of life with this book. I would rather have written "A Chaste Man" than any novel of Dreiser save "Sister Carrie," and Wilkinson's heroine Olga is an even finer creation than Carrie. I have always faith in the future of a man who can paint women to the life. Besides, Wilkinson's style is excellent—simple, sincere, but touched now and again to beauty. Here is a sentence: "She stood before him with her rich young head drooped and her child's figure a little swaying"—that rich" is pure magic.

Wilkinson's latest book is perhaps his best. "Brute Gods" deserves to be read very carefully even by those who think themselves masters of the story-telling art.

I do not by this mean that the book as a whole is well told or well constructed. It is not. In the beginning we have a family lightly sketched, the wife and mother has run away with a lover and as soon as we get to know the father and husband we understand why any woman would run away from him.

What makes the book is the description of the love of a boy of nineteen, Alec, for Gillian Collett, a woman six or seven years older than himself, who is rather ashamed of carrying on with a boy, and yet is seduced time and again by the boy's passionate desire and whole-hearted abandonment to his affection. The older woman tries to feel cynical towards the youth, but she cannot; his passionate admiration is too sweet to her; in spite of herself she yields more and more to him. Here is a page I must reproduce; for it seems to me of extraordinary quality:

" 'You're wonderful'." He was close to her, he spoke low. " 'I don't know—I didn't know that any one could be so—' "

" 'Oh, I'm not! You can't really—I mean you don't know me at all!' "

"Her arms dropped, she wavered before him. His look of utmost conviction shamed her words. That religious look of a devotee, it was absorbingly new to her, yet not new, she had in some sort known it. It was terrible that he should be so sure, that his youth should do this to him; it was terrible, and great. That strong eagerness of his mouth, his eyes so darkly lit, his boyish candor, all his unknowing boldness . . . she could have dropped at his feet and humbled herself to him forever. No other way but to hold fast by that tenderness and passion. He could subdue her, this boy who seemed to be at her will.

" 'I want you!' " he whispered. " 'You can't tell how much—I must—' "

" 'But what?' " She held out her hands, and he caught them, burning her through.

" 'It's not like anything I've ever—it's because—Oh, I—I love you! May I say that, do you mind? do you?' "

"Her mouth shook, she waited for him to say it again.

" 'May I kiss you?' "

"The girl of twenty-six was wholly taken by that question which no one but a novice can ever ask. The contrast of his diffidence and humility and restraint with the overpowering and momentous compulsion that drove from him, so sure in his mouth and eyes, confirmed her his. She did not answer, she looked hard, then she kissed him, and stayed."

No one living, it seems to me, except Louis Wilkinson, could have written this page, and it is better than anything he has done so far. It ranks to me with that short-story of Galsworthy's, "The Apple Tree," which I have praised in and out of season. It is as fine even as Galsworthy's and, if anything, better realized, and more intimate, though not so well expressed. One could almost swear it was a personal experience of Wilkinson's. If he had deliberately written the book round this incident between the boy and the woman I think he would have made the book a classic. As it is I am not straining eulogy when I say he has written some pages that anyone might be proud to sign.

It seems to me everything may be hoped from such beginnings. Wilkinson has as much temperament as W. L. George and knows not only France and French but classic literature as well and America to boot. His roots strike deep and are richly nourished.

He has kept his head perfectly throughout the war; without making himself conspicuous by kicking against the pricks he has yet never concealed his frank opinion that English policy was at least as selfish and sordid as that of Germany and that all the combatants deserve to lose for embarking on a war that could benefit no one. His opinion of the Peace and the League of Nations is not flattering either to Lloyd George, Clemenceau or President Wilson. I find in him high qualities both of intellect and character. I have only known him personally for the last three years here in New York; but to me he is both likeable and interesting. In person very tall, just over six feet I should think, and slight, but giving one the impression of wiry strength. His manner is that of the student, reflective and retiring rather than brisk or ready, yet he talks excellently when you know him and has neither false modesty nor undue shyness.

He writes me that he has accepted a position offered to him in England and is not likely therefore to return to these States for some years. I regard that as a piece of good fortune for him; the scene of all his stories is laid in England. The creative artist needs a special *terroir;* it is not good for him to become too cosmopolitan; we only grow to be masters of ordinary life and ordinary men and women by living much with them.

I expect considerable things from Wilkinson; in both "A Chaste Man" and "Brute Gods" the story is not at once as clear as I think it should be; it dawns on you after a while and becomes plain enough; but one is a little perplexed and irritated just at first and this is a fault to be shunned, not repeated. I want his next story to begin as simply and persuasively as *"The Cloister and the Hearth,"* or *"Le Curé de Tours"* and then I shall settle myself down for an hour's pure enjoyment. Wilkinson has the heart of the matter in him I am persuaded and so I bid him gird up his loins and give us his very best.

W. L. George

## W. L. GEORGE

THE first time I met W. L. George was some ten years ago at an an artistic "At Home" in Chelsea. He made a pleasant impression; a strong, well set-up figure, some five feet nine or ten in height, with dark handsome face; a courteous mannr with a suspicion of self-assurance that announced to me the coming generation. Just as we of the Fifties met the Brownings and Arnolds of the Twenties and Thirties, so now the young men born in the Eighties came to dispute with us the pride of place. George met me on even footing, He was willing enough to listen, but I soon had occasion to remark that he knew French thoroughly and spoke it like a native. His book on "France in the Twentieth Century" had not impressed me deeply. It was good honest journeyman's work far ahead of average British opinion in knowledge, but not subtle or imaginative or complete; the heights in French life unexplored; he never mentioned Descartes or Pascal, Vauvenargues or Verlaine; his outlook was that of a journalist rather than that of a thinker or poet, and because of this feeling of mine that he lived on the surface I was inclined to resent a little his self-confidence. Suddenly I was asked by some one to notice that Mrs. George was smoking a pipe or it may have been a cigar. In any case attention was drawn to the couple rather by force than by charm.

A year or so afterwards the town was startled by "A

Bed of Roses." The thesis, if I remember it rightly, was that a woman might find a "gay" life more amusing and more lucrative than a humdrum existence. But there were moments in the novel of soul-analysis sufficient to redeem a worse subject, and one had to admit that George had studied or absorbed certain types of women with rare insight. He was not as successful in his portraits of men, but on the whole one felt that a new novelist had made a successful first appearance.

I am not sure that his later books have bettered his position greatly. "The Second Blooming" seems to me the best of them, and indeed the story of the wife's seduction, which is the theme of that book, is excellently managed, while the subsequent love-passages and the final breaking-off are all realistically realized and rendered with French fairness. But there is nothing in the book that takes the breath like the love-idyll in Richard Feverel. There is no charm in it to be compared to the charm of Galsworthy's little story entitled "The Apple Tree." George gives us a picture of love and passion, but nowhere ecstacy or the magic of lyric vision.

"Blind Alley" is another love story which this time comes to nothing, and is therefore not so interesting as "The Second Blooming." Nor is the feminine psychology of the book quite so deep; the scalpel is not used so boldly; the nerves are not laid bare so dexterously.

Of all George's books "The Making of an Englishman" or "The Little Beloved," as it is entitled by Little, Brown & Co. of Boston, the American publishers, is the one that throws most light on the author's mentality and temperament. It is the story of a young Frenchman who comes to London and goes into business to make a fortune. But we are told little of his adventures in the city and much about his landlady's two daughters, and especially about the eldest daughter Maud, who is quite willing to kiss and flirt with the young Frenchman, but will not go any further unless he's minded to marry.

Maud is a really brilliant study of a sound-hearted, self-interested girl of the lower middle class of Cockaigne who is perfectly well able to take care of herself in any circumstances. Maud evades the attack and the young Frenchman is bitterly disappointed, but he turns at once to a daughter of his employer, "Edith" who shows him another side of English character.

Edith is a girl of the better class, romantic, affectionate and very pretty, and the Frenchman falls in love with her bit by bit, for like most Frenchman, and most young men for that matter, he is "in love with love," and on the quest of it perpetually.

These two studies of contrasted English types, Maud and Edith, are as good as anything George has done or indeed seems likely to do.

George's political views strike one as rather shallow. He has interspersed them through the love story and they come rather to irritate us like thin editorials, and yet they are fair-minded enough in a certain way.

He tells us on one page that the cry of Home Rule arouses "troublesome memories" in him, and that "the English tricks in Egypt, South Africa and Ireland annoy him.' He tries hard to be liberal without any deep comprehension of the struggle going on underneath the surface betrween the Haves and the Have-Nots, which is, as Goethe saw a hundred years ago, the real, the vital problem of the modern world.

George's views on politics are nothing like so interesting as his views of women. He is by nature a lover. He has studied love from the man's point of view with passionate earnestness, and so every now and then has caught glimpses of the woman's view of the matter, glimpses and gleams which light up his pages. The story of his bethrothal to Edith and her father's opinion of the matter, and his final success complete "The Making of an Englishman," and the whole book is, as I have said, extremely interesting.

Whether George will ever write a masterpiece or not, would be very difficult indeed to determine. He has it in him to write a great love story, but he must take, I think, time for it and give his real knowledge of man's and woman's passions generous opportunities. All one can say at the moment is that he has the root of the matter in him. He feels passionately, writes excellently and is not afraid to say what he feels. One must simply hope for the best and wait.

Scattered up and down his books are phrases which stick in the memory. "There is no place like home," he says, and then adds, "which is one comfort." He paints a bishop pleading for national organization and discipline by suggesting that the bishop means to do the organization while the rest of the world will come in for the discipline. And finally he sums up his own creed, the last sentence of which is almost a proof of genius:

"Work sixteen hours a day. During the other eight dream of your work. Check your references three times; then get somebody to check them again. Collect all the facts you can; then realize there are some you don't know. Acquire strong convictions; then doubt them. In other words, keep your mind fluid, so that always it may be fit to flow into the most obscure crannies of human singularity."

An excellent program: but you can only keep your mind "fluid" by cultivating your sympathies. It is by the heart we grow, and all our deepest thoughts come from the heart.

George is about forty with an established reputation and a lazy, carefree life assured with even four hours' work a day. What will he do? His French education and training gave him a splendid start and he used it to the uttermost; but now? Has he laid broad bases for eternity? Who shall say?

After forty with reputation made we are not apt to learn much. Is George growing? I don't know. His scattered remarks on the war have been much more central, less provincial I mean, than those of Wells and Bennett; his French training saved him from the worst extravagances; but something more is needed for enduring fame. A great mental effort or a great passion, or a supreme self-sacrifice—many are the ways; but daemonic power is the first requirement of that I see no trace.

Henri Gaudier-Brzeska

# GAUDIER-BRZESKA

WE are living in a rebirth of religion and of art, comparable only to the Reformation and the Renaissance of art in the sixteenth century. But in the upheaval of three centuries ago, thought led the way and art followed after, whereas now the spring of art is passing into high summer, while the new thought is putting timidly forth the first bourgeonings. It is difficult to fix exactly the beginnings of great movements. Nine out of ten observers would give the credit of this rebirth of art to France and trace the growth through Delacroix, to the Barbizon school and so to Cézanne, the epoch-making initiator who was followed by Picasso, Gaudier-Brzeska, Epstein, Wyndham Lewis and the rest. Just as the first renaissance was caused by the fall of Constantinople and the consequent influx of learned Greeks into Italy who brought with them Greek letters and models of Greek sculpture, so this modern renaissance was caused, or at least quickened by the discovery of the paintings and pottery of China and the prints and pictures of the Japanese, by Indian and Persian miniatures too, and sculptures from all parts of the world and of all times. The Goncourts in France and Whistler in England were among the first to assimilate some of these new influences. They were the first to teach that every art had its own domain, its own laws, its own home in the spirit, the first to reject the influence of literature on painting, or of the pictorial art on the literary art; the first to question Shakespeare's statement that art was there "to hold the mirror up to nature." They despised the mere representation of the actual and demanded an interpretation; some even attempted as the old Chinese sage advised to leave reality altogether, in order more freely to suggest "the rhythm of things."

The mark of the new movement is boldness and sincerity. Picasso is not afraid to recall the austerity and menace of a Spanish hilltown by a series of cubes posed one above the other as roof on roof, and his superb success gave a name to the new departure and induced others to try to evoke the soft curves of feminine beauty by cubes and parallelograms of rectangular harshness. But the successes grew more and more numerous; Gauguin's picture of Christ in Gethsemane was declared to be a masterpiece by the masters, while the so-called critics denounced it as a blasphemy or an absurdity. The Garden was a rough incult olive wood with carious soil sparsely covered with bunches of coarse grass; here on a bank the Teacher sits who could not let ill alone; his head bowed in utter dejection; the face livid with despair and apprehension and against the graygreen skin a hemisphere of scarlet hair—and this flaming color, never seen on human head before, suggests the supernatural, is in itself an evocation of the ineffable that lifts this tragedy above all others in recorded time.

Here is a woman's figure by Matisse; a few bold curves, the utmost simplification of line and yet the soft warmth and weight of the flesh is on our fingers with a magic of suggestion that no Venus, whether of Cnidos or of Paris, ever before called forth. Matisse, we know, was a masterdraughtsman or he could not thus seize on the essential, omitting everything else.

Curiously enough this simplification of means and sincerity of feeling alike led the artist to primitive schools of design and modeling. We had all passed in the British Museum from the Parthenon sculptures to the Assyrian and from the recognized schools to ignored or unnoted efforts of so-called savages. There are sculptures from Gambogia in the Trocadero in Paris as magnificent in their own way as the greatest Chinese paintings.

These things were in my mind when one afternoon I was introduced in a friend's room to a young man, Gaudier-Brzeska. I was struck at once by Gaudier's sharp thin profile and his quick incisive way of speaking. He was below rather than above medium height; slight but strong; he had a little down curling carelessly about his chin and this with his bold out-jutting nose and keen round brown eyes gave him an old-world appearance. He looked like a young Italian artist of the Renaissance and I soon found he had all the true artist's enthusiasm. I took a great fancy to him because of the outspoken frankness of his criticism and asked him to call. He promised to, but a couple of days later I met him again. I happened to be in the British Museum looking about among the cases containing the idols and art-products of the South Sea islanders; suddenly Gaudier-Brzeska appeared and pointing to a figurine a span long said:

"Gaudy, isn't it? More wonderful than the sisters of Pheidias."

"What are you doing here?" I cried.

"I often come here," he answered with that peculiar mixture of shyness and of self-assertion which was a note of him; "there are masterpieces here of all sorts; look at that and that! The splendor of them!" His English was always more expressive than correct.

I nodded; "I wish I could handle them," he added.

"Come downstairs," he burst out, "where they keep the early Assyrian things—statues finer far than any of Greece."

The haste, the passionate exaggeration, the staccato utterance, were characteristic of his youth, I thought; surely the frankest, sincerest, most assured nature I have ever met.

I went with him and on the way, "Why do you run down the Greeks?" I asked, "Rodin declares that they were the master artists of the world."

Guadier pursed out his lips in contempt and shrugged his shoulders:

"What do I care? Rodin is one man, I am another."

"I have always thought the Greeks very young," I continued, "satisfied with the sensuous appeal in the beautiful naked form of man and woman."

"That's it," he cried; "or part of it; they never expressed anything but sex, but here you're got my Assyrian who expresses spiritual qualities and characters with an extraordinary simplicity of means."

I have always thought his own bust of Ezra Pound was the creative equivalent of his critical appreciation of the great Primitives. At any rate, it is the best symbol I can recall of Gaudier's meaning. He was never tired of directing attention to the soft outlines of the early masters; no sharp line; no black shadow, just a shade; every outline wavering in a sort of haze and the features simplified, to the uttermost, only indicated indeed, yet infinitely suggestive.

His method and message were both new and of a passionate, searching sincerity; again and again he tried to define his position; "the modern sculptor is a man who works with instinct as his inspiring force. His work is emotional. What he feels, he feels intensely; and his work is the abstraction of this intense feeling."

The creative artist is usually concrete, all in images and pictures; but here was one seeking to give form to abstractions.

I began to realize that young Brzeska had something definite and new to express, though words and especially English words were evidently not his medium. Talking with me he usually lapsed into French; but even there he found it hard to render his abstract thought.

The first thing that impressed me in Gaudier was his speed, an unearthly quickness of perception and reaction. He was a sort of shy, wild, faun-like creature all in exclamations and interjections, this moment in passionate enthusiasm, oftener in passionate contempt. But always astoundingly intelligent, always intensely alive and eager, tireless, indeed, in his intellectual demands. He aston-

THE HORSE
Progressive studies in the relation of masses
By Henri Gaudier-Brzeska

ished me once by his knowledge of German. "Where did you learn it?" I asked.

"In Munich," he replied; "I went there from Bristol." At fourteen, it appeared, he had won a traveling scholarship in his native France which gave him two years in a college in Bristol and in Bristol he won a scholarship that took him to Munich.

"How did you live there?" I queried.

"By drawing Rembrandt heads of Jews," he grinned, "another man used to paint them and then a third would tone the papier with tea extract till our Rembrandt was good enough to sign and sell in America," and he laughed impishly.

After knowing him a month or so, I went with him to his studio in Putney; it was one bare room of a dozen side by side.

"Whistler once worked here somewhere," I remarked.

"It's no worse for that," retorted Gaudier and we both laughed at the cheeky retort.

The first five minutes spent in his studio convinced me of Gaudier's genius. There were drawings on the walls of torsos; a picture of a wicker-basket full of apples, as as good as any still-life of Cézanne or Picasso, and done in the same flat colors without shading. In spite of my poverty I bought it on the spot. Everywhere there were curious modelings in clay, carvings in stone; notably a high-relief of two men side by side gazing with greedy long eyes at a seated girl. Like most of his sculptures, this was colored and had a sort of sensual heat in it strangely impressive.

The mark of the youth was always intelligence, incisive self-assurance, and modernity of interest and view. He knew a good deal of modern French poetry by heart; but I never heard him quote anyone earlier than Baudelaire except Villon; indeed, Villon and Verlaine, Bruand and Jehan Rictus were his favorites. He knew a verse or two of Goethe, half a dozen or so of Heine and he believed or pretended to believe that was all that could be found in German.

His self-confidence provoked me once to try to "draw" him, in order to define his limitations; but his sincerity and intelligence carried him over the test triumphantly.

"Why on earth did you select sculpture," I asked, "which is one of the simplest of the arts, instead of painting, for which you are at least as gifted, or poetry, which is the highest of the arts because the most complex?"

"Poetry," he barked. "Pooh! All the new work is being done by the sculptors and painters. Where have you an interpretation in poetry? The poets are all working just as their forefathers worked five centuries ago; but we are doing new stuff."

"What nonsense," I exclaimed. "A century before Cézanne, William Blake did the best impressionist work ever seen."

"Blake?" he asked, evidently not knowing even the name.

"William Blake," I replied, "who did an impressionist landscape of evening before any of the modern painters were heard of. About 1775 at the age of sixteen he wrote:

> The night wind sleeps upon the lake,
> Come Silence with thy glimmering eyes and wash
> The dusk with silver.

And what do you think of his famous 'Tiger,' the greatest of lyrics, I think; at least the most epochmaking and eventful ever written:

> Tiger, Tiger, burning bright
> In the forests of the night.
> What immortal hand or eye
> Framed thy dreadful symmetry?

No representation, here: no description; nothing but the imaginative symbol: you remember?"

"No, no!" he cried, "I never heard it before; but how magnificent! Do go on, please," and I was forced willy-nilly to recite the whole poem.

"Good God," he exclaimed when I had finished, "who would have believed that an Englishman could have got there in the eighteenth century? It's simply incredible. Did he do anything more of that class?"

"Sure," I replied, "and higher stuff still; he was of the prophet-seers worthy to stand with the greatest, with Shakespeare and Jesus."

The name served to excite him. "Jesus," he burst out, "was *contre le nationalisme;* that was all He did, His only title to honor."

"Whew!" I whistled. "Your creative work is better than your criticism, my young friend, or I wouldn't waste my time with you. You are to be forgiven, though; you only deny the Blakes and the Christs because you don't know them."

"Lend me Blake?" he asked shyly.

"Of course, with pleasure,' I replied, "it is more yours than mine as you want it more," and I handed him a volume.

Henri Gaudier was perfectly simple and frank on all

DEER
(Pen Drawing)
By Henri Gaudier-Brzeska

occasions; met prince and peasant on the same even footing; was careless of dress and appearance; would fill his pockets with carvings and carry a heavy piece of marble slung over his shoulder down Piccadilly in the afternoon without being in the slightest self-conscious. In other words, he had no vanity.

Leaving his studio after that first visit, I thought of

him as a most characteristic product of our time; an artist of our renaissance. He was very proud; though always hard up, often too poor to buy marble except in scraps, he never asked for loans or favors.

When I first knew him, he told me he had a clerkship in the city which gave him and his sister a bare livelihood; but as soon as he got to know a few people and had sold half a dozen pieces of sculpture he threw up the clerkship and tried to live on his earnings as an artist. he could live easily, he said, on a couple of pounds a week and when I knew he was getting more than that I dismissed the matter from my mind as settled satisfactorily.

But one day shortly before I came to grief myself I realized that he was in difficulties. He declared that a bookseller to whom he had intrusted some of his sculptures was cheating him: "He laughs and laughs," he said, "and sticks to all the money he gets from selling my works, and I can hardly live. I must get back to France. I left it because I didn't want to waste time serving in the army. If it were not for that, I'd go back to-morrow. It's easier for an artist to live in France . . . Paris," he added with a sort of passionate longing.

I could not but admit that he was right.

Six months later the war broke out and after some natural hesitations he returned to France, was promptly arrested for having evaded service and was imprisoned. He broke gaol at Calais within a few hours and managed to return to London. But the call was in his blood and his fate was upon him. He went to his Embassy, won Paul Cambon's good word and returned to France to be enrolled promptly. In due time he was sent to the front. He bore all the hardships of life in the trenches with smiling good humor, took the rough with the smooth, and in six months was made a corporal. Again and again he declared that he would survive the war he was "absolutely sure," but it was youth and the spring of blood in him that spoke; he was shot through the forehead in a charge at Neuville St. Vaast, June 5, 1915, after two promotions for gallantry.

Mr. Ezra Pound, the poet, tells the truth about the catastrophe when he says that the killing of Gaudier-Brzeska was a greater loss to humanity than the destruction of the cathedral at Rheims. The great church was known and had been assimilated by thousands; what Gaudier had in him to give, no one now can ever know; but speaking for myself, I must say that I expected greater things from him than from any young man I have ever met.

Let me give now a few extracts from his letters at the front just to give an idea of the boyish good-humor and manliness that distinguished this rare artist.

"The beastly regiment which was here before us remained three months, and as they were all dirty northern miners used to all kind of dampness, they never did an effort to better the place up a bit. When we took the trenches after the march it was a sight worthy of Dante; there was at the bottom a foot deep of liquid mud in which we had to stand two days and two nights, rest we had in small holes nearly as muddy, add to this a position making a V point into the enemy who shells us from three sides, the close vicinity of 800 putrefying German corpses, and you are at the front in the marshes of the Aisne. . . . .

"Our woods are magnificent. I am just now quartered in trenches in the middle of them, they are covered with lily of the valley, it grows and flowers on the trench itself. In the night we have many nightingales to keep us company. They sing very finely and the loud noise of the usual attacks and counterattacks does not disturb them in the least.

"It is very warm and nice out of doors, one does not mind sleeping out on the ground now."

And the combative stuff with the magnificent summing up as noble as a judgement of Goethe.

"We give them nice gas to breathe when the wind is for us. I have magnificent little bombs, they are as big as an ostrich egg, they smell of ripe apples, but when they burst your eyes weep until you can't see, you are suffocated, and if the *boche* wants to save his skin he has to scoot. Then a good little bullet puts an end to his misery. This is not war, but a murderer hunt, we have to bring these rascals out of their holes, we do it and kill them remorselessly when they do not surrender.

"To-day is magnificent, a fresh wind, clear sun and larks singing cheerfully. The shells do not disturb the songsters. In the Champagne woods the nightingales took no notice of the fight either. They solemnly proclaim man's foolery and sacrilege of nature. I respect their disdain."

The best collection of Brzeska's works is owned by Mr. John Quinn, the famous New York lawyer. Mr. Pound in his delightful book gives us part of the letter which Mr. Quinn wrote on hearing of poor Gaudier's death:

"Now here is the distressing thing to me personally. I got yours of April 18th on May 10th. It was mostly about Brzeska's work. I intended to write and send you twenty pounds or thirty pounds, and say, 'Send this to him and say it can go on account of whatever you select for me.' But a phrase of yours stuck in my mind, that when he came back from the trenches he would be hard up. Poor brave fellow. There is only the memory now of a brave gifted man. What I can do I will do."

I quote this because Mr. Quinn is one of the few collectors who realize that if a man buys the work of artists who need money to go on with, he in some measure shares in the creation. He gives the man leisure for work.

Taken all in all Gaudier was the largest and best endowed artist I have known. As resolute and brave as a born man of action, proud and self-reliant too and yet artist to his finger-tips, as gifted for painting as for sculpture and with an imperial intelligence. What might he not have done?—a great man, superbly endowed!

When people compare him with Rodin depreciatingly, I get angry. Rodin has done his work and done it magnificently; but Gaudier had both hands full of new gifts and was aflame to give of his best—richer gifts, I verily believe, than any sculptor since Angelo, and there is some justification for my faith; here and there a cut stone of supreme excellence, as beautiful as a Shakespeare sonnet, but, alas, Gaudier died at twenty-four, his splendid promise half-fulfilled! For me he stands at the head of all the millions of brave men who have perished untimely in this dreadful war; I can still see the eager face and lamping eyes and hear the quick stabbing exclamations— ah, the pity of it, the pity of it! the untimely shrouding of that victorious intelligence!

Lord St. Aldwyn

# EARL ST. ALDWYN

IT was in 1887, I believe, that I first made the acquaintance of Sir Michael Hicks-Beach; at any rate it was just after he had resigned his position as Chief Secretary for Ireland. It was said that a serious affection of his eyes had forced him to give up all work. But that was regarded as a convenient pretext to cover failure and defeat.

The whole position throws such light on British politics and on the character of a great man who has been persistently misunderstood and underrated that now Michael Hicks-Beach is dead, I may be forgiven for sketching it summarily.

It was his amendment to the Budget that had brought about the defeat of Gladstone's government in 1885. Already in 1878 Hicks-Beach had been Secretary for the Colonies; later he had startled people by imperious manners more than by any originality of view. For him to accept the Chief Secretaryship and risk a growing fame in Dublin—"That grave of English reputations" was looked upon as a weakness—or at least an admission that he could not get his own price from his party. His enemies chuckled: "An eclipse, . . . the finish."

Some of us who rather liked what we had seen of the man held our breath; the risk was appalling! Why had he thrown himself into the abyss? For Ireland was at boiling point: Parnell, one of the greatest of men had drawn the sword and thrown the scabbard away: "No rent" was being muttered and screamed and shouted from Donegal to Cork: English landlordism snarled with bared teeth behind its lawfences: a dozen able men, chief among them Tim Healy, were attacking night after night in the House of Commons with unrivalled sarcasm and passionate contempt: England, obstinate, glowering, was set against all rebels—yet ominous mutterings were heard that Ulster was being won by the "no-rent" bait, the last English stronghold disaffected: anything might happen.

Into the caldron plunged Hicks-Beach, a tall, dour, imperious Englishman, a Conservative, a landlord of the narrowest landlord class, a country gentleman—Eton and Oxford: nature, traditions, education—all against him, said the wise: would it end in another tragedy, the torch hiss out in blood as it had gone out six years before? We waited, hardly daring to hope.

The turmoil in Ireland went on though dulled and damped, we thought: the Irish leaders hesitating, watching. Then to our wonder, *The Times* began gravely to warn the Chief Secretary! He was hesitant, it appeared, weak; (we grinned—that was not his failing!) he was adjured to act boldly against the lawbreakers, the rebels. Our hearts beat high again with hope. The other English papers began to copy *The Times*. *The Times* went on to scold and then to curse, shriller and shriller, day after day, while the cry joined in, the whole pack, now their pockets were threatened, squealing, cursing, threatening:

the London Clubs all in a fury; then the word—"Hicks-Beach, the traitor!"

After six months, the issue at length; clear, definite for all men to see and take sides according to the God or the Devil in them! Only great men bring about such crises! Lord Clanricarde, of evil fame, the worst of absentee landlords, wrote to *The Times* to say that he had called upon the forces of the Crown to protect the officers of the law who were collecting his rents, long overdue.

The Chief Secretary had replied in contempt of law: "I refuse absolutely to use the forces of the Crown to collect Lord Clanricarde's debts." Nothing more, no explanation, even, just that, signed "Hicks-Beach."

The sensation was indescribable. London went crazy. You might have thought a piece of the sky had fallen. For the second time in its record of over a century *The Times* devoted two leading articles in one morning to one subject. In the first it condemned Hicks-Beach root and branch: he had gone outside his powers; he was one of the executive appointed to carry out the laws, not to make laws and bring in anarchy: his intellect, always overrated by himself, must be temporarily deranged. In the second diatribe it was shown quietly that in refusing to collect Clanricarde's debts, he was judging and sentencing Lord Clanricarde without even hearing him; in the present state of Ireland he was going further, making war on all credit, on property itself—property, the corner-stone of civilization, property, the keystone of the arch that bridges the abyss from barbarism to a state of order—trained rhetoric of the Devil's advocates.

The Times won and won easily. Even the London Liberal papers would not take up cudgels for a Conservative who had done what they did not dare even to preach. They had condemned the Irish for refusing to pay rent: how could they applaud this English Conservative squire who refused to collect debts, as his duty bade him? The Irish waited and watched!

Suddenly the news was published that Hicks-Beach's eyes having given out through stress of work he had resigned and returned to London to be doctored. *The Times* was not even jubilant or self-gratulatory. The outcome was the only possible one: "England is a law-abiding country." The Clubs, every one, said that Hicks-Beach was ruined and would never be heard of again. "He should go back to his country-place, Coln St. Aldwyn and grow turnips."

It was at this moment I met him. The dinner was given by the celebrated doctor, Robson Roose, and in his invitation he told me that Lord Randolph Churchill was to be there and other Cabinet Ministers. Would I please come early, he wanted to introduce me to Sir Michael Hicks-Beach? I accepted eagerly. I wanted to meet and measure the man who had acted so boldly, so foolishly, so nobly. Had he been swayed by moral or by intellectual motives?

Robson Roose took me into a small room off the dining-room. Sir Michael Hicks-Beach was standing at the fireplace with his back to us. As we entered and Robson Roose mentioned his name he turned slowly. He had a heavy shade over his eyes and looked worn and thin, I thought.

"I am so glad to meet you," I said and as Robson left the room, I added, "I should say so 'proud'."

"Really!" he said in a tired voice ending in a sound, half sniff, half snort, "not many persons would say that!"

"You didn't act hoping for the applause of the many."

"Indeed, no!" he cried. "I knew better than that."

"The curious thing about the business is," I went on, "that you acted as the moral conscience of the English people and thus settled the Irish question. Your honesty and courage will have great results—do infinite good."

In silence he turned to me with his face all working and held out his hand. In a moment he had regained control of himself though the tears were on his cheeks. He took out his handkerchief and wiped them away openly. Then in a half-voice:

"Thank you! I shall always remember that. *That* makes me proud. That was what I said to myself. One's conscience the only compass-light in bad weather," he added smiling. Sea-similes came naturally even to the country squire's lips, for all Englishmen are of sailor-stock.

"Of course you knew how they would treat you?' I went on.

He nodded: "None of my business"—curtly—"I had to show 'em that England, the England I love, did not mean to go on doing wrong. I'm glad," he added, "that you think it will have a good effect ultimately. So far, it appears to have had no consequences except to throw me out!" he added bitterly.

"Consequences are incalculable," I said. "The act brought me to you, eager to help. It will bring dozens of others, as Cromwell used to say 'a small band of good men,' standing on this because they cannot help it—*an invisible cloud of witnesses!* You'll come back triumphant!"

"Come back," he repeated, resuming a conventional tone, as our host accompanied by others entered the room, "I must first go away to Coln and get cured. A tedious job, I'm afraid."

Our talk was ended. At the dinner he hardly spoke at all. As soon as it was over, he took Robson Roose into another room and disappeared.

We met the next time in the inner lobby of the House of Commons. He stopped and came over to me and shook hands.

"Yes, the eyes are better," he said, "much better, thank you and thanks to you in some part for what you said."

Next year, 1888, Hicks-Beach returned to the House of Commons, eyes cured, health completely reëstablished. His originality had not cost him his influence with his party, for he was at once made President of the Board of Trade, and held the office till the Liberals returned to power in 1902.

In those three years he fulfilled the hopes of his friends and grounded his reputation; he won the permanent officials in his department, and became known as **an able administrator.**

In 1905 the Conservatives again carried the elections and Hicks-Beach was appointed Chancellor of the Exchequer, the highest office in the government after that of Prime Minister.

Twenty years before, at fifty, he had been leader of the House for a short time. He had a certain curt abruptness of manner, the outward and visible sign in him of an aloofness of mind, which the ordinary member of Parliament resented, regarded as unjustifiable conceit in one who was hardly more than a poor baronet, a country squire. Some one, annoyed by his imperiousness, called him "Black Michael." I think Swift MacNeil was the godfather, and the nickname showed extraordinary divination, for it was not suggested by appearance. Sir Michael Hicks-Beach was tall, about six feet in height, and wore a short, brown beard; his face was rather long, his head long, too. At fifty he looked forty and was neither dark nor fair: why, then, Black Michael?

Throughout his dark days of pain and neglect the nickname was unused, yet it was curiously appropriate and forecast the future. The contempt Hicks-Beach felt for the party that threw him over in 1887, when as Irish Secretary he had acted to the highest in him, left its mark, reinforcing his natural melancholy. At the Board of Trade he did his work and kept to himself and the consciousness of power grew upon him. Always proud and self-centered, he became prouder and more accustomed to trust his own judgement, as he saw how his ablest subordinates had to bow to it.

Now, at nearly seventy, he took up the work of

Chancellor of the Exchequer, feeling sure that the higher the pedestal, the better his height would be appreciated. Even before his first Budget he surprised the House by taking a line of his own again and again in debate. There was insight in the man which gave him new expressions. Never fluent, much less rhetorical, regarded, indeed, as somewhat inarticulate, he yet coined the phrase "the open door" in China, which stuck and was adopted in both Germany and France. Impartial observers began to revise their previous superficial estimate of him, began to wonder whether by any chance Hicks-Beach was a great man. His first Budget deepened the high opinion of him which was again being put forward by permanent officials of the department. He got up in a crowded House and without a trace of hesitancy or of preparation put forth the annual balance-sheet with a clearness and mastery of figures that surprised every one. He hardly used a note. He stood there, a tall, lean man, doing his job, without frills of any sort, without waiting for applause or even noticing it when it came. He ended in the same conversational way by declaring that in an English Treasury official, parsimony was the chiefest virtue: waste the ordinary democratic pitfall. No rule, however, without exceptions; reluctantly he had borrowed from the Sinking Fund; he would do so again if necessary: no canons holy, no command sacred in a rich and growing concern—save economy.

The curt phrases, the command of the position, the even strong voice, never loud, always clear, the conversational tone, had an astonishing effect: "very able . . . a big man" was the verdict of those capable of judging.

Next morning the papers praised him almost without reserve. Some critics in the House next night tried to pick holes. He listened in silence till the last one had aired his fad and then got up and declared he had only heard one thing worth noticing in the four hours. He dealt with the objection like a master and then walked out of the House as if he did not care a copper what the Members thought of him. Suddenly every one spoke f him as "Black Michael": his daring to speak the truth, his felt disdain, the underlying pessimism and melancholy justified the nickname.

But there was deep and generous kindliness in the man besides imperious strength. I went to see him shortly before his second Budget. Every one was excited about it; the South African War had cost a great deal; the recovery after it was surprisingly slow; thinking men were beginning to realize the new truth that half of all the wealth of a country is produced every year, that money spent on powder and shot is worse than thrown away, that unproductive production is more wasteful than unproductive consumption; in fine, that fighting costs more than money and luxuries must be paid for twice over.

I found that though Hicks-Beach hadn't read much political economy, he had grasped essentials, approaching every question from the moral side, found them all surprisingly simple. Again and again he emphasized the need of economy: "Can't have your cake and eat it . . . the whole country wanted the war, now they must pay for it . . . war usually idiotic. . . . Chamberlain too combative."

When the talk was over I asked him might I use what he had told me in my paper. He got up and whistled:

"Whew! What would the House say if I gave the Budget provisions first to a newspaper . . ." He smiled, shaking his head. "I'm afraid that's impossible."

"But my paper is so small." I replied, "it would have little importance . . . every one in power would pretend not to believe it . . . many would think I was forecasting the future from the past." He still shook his head, smiling. I had not found the true argument. Again I tried:

"Nothing you have told me would have any effect on the Stock Exchange. I shall expect you to deny that you gave it to me for publication." Quickly he rejoined:

"No, no, I sha'n't disavow you; I want to help you. H'm, h'm . . . What you say about the Stock Exchange is true. That's the real reason such things are kept secret and divulged to the House first." A moment's thought and suddenly he exclaimed: "Go ahead: tell it all; I don't care, let 'em grumble, d—n them."

I got up at once, fearing second thoughts, and possible reservations; but he had dismissed the subject from his mind.

"You keep as young looking as ever," he remarked pleasantly. "How do you manage it? You look thirty, yet you must be near fifty?"

"More," I replied, laughing. "I could return the compliment; you look fifty, and yet . . ."

"Seventy, seventy," he repeated. "Three score years and ten . . . I'll soon say vixi," he added half-bitterly.

The only expression in a foreign language I ever heard him use; struck by it probably at Eton—"I have lived."

I looked at his face: it was worn; lines everywhere: deep-set, sad eyes, as if they shrank from seeing life stripped of youth's roseate glamour.

"Lots still to do," I cried. "The last fight, the best."

"Curious," he exclaimed, putting his hands on my shoulders. "You say the things I've been saying to myself. There may still be something worth fighting for," he mused . . . and we parted.

The result justified my guess. I published the three chief provisions of the Budget and they appeared in print and on posters all over London some days before Hicks-Beach made his Budget speech in the House; but no paper took any notice of the pronouncement. It did me some good and no one any harm.

One Irishman in the House remarked that he seemed to have heard Hicks-Beach's speech before: "the provisions of it were in the air, so to speak": the pin-prick made members smile.

Some years later a proposal to take Salisbury Plain for army manœuvers on a grand scale passed the House of Commons. The landlords had to be bought out: their lands therefore were valued and the contest between so-called private rights and national needs began. As usual in England the nation's pocket suffered. When the private telegraph companies were taken over by the post-office the state had to pay three times their real value.

So now the landowners held out for and obtained three prices and more for every acre of land the government wanted. Michael Hicks-Beach, now Lord St. Aldwyn, owned a small slice of Salisbury Plain. I believe about 33 acres. When it came to bargaining for it, he asked, I think, £163,000, and was stiff against any reduction.

The matter came up in the House of Commons: some Liberal had stumbled on the "pot of roses," or more probably the Liberal Chancellor of the Exchequer took care that the secret should be known in order to show how much more honest he was than his Conservative predecessor. However this may be, the question was put and his answer was:

"Yes, Lord St. Aldwyn asked and received £163,500 for thirty-three acres." (I can't be sure of the exact amount.)

Members looked at each other: the price was incredibly high.

The next question was even more illuminating: What was the government valuation? The answer came pat £13,500."

The effect was stunning: no hypocritical veil could resist such a stab. Suddenly a whisper—"Black Michael had taken £150,000 exactly to keep his peerage on"— a smile on every face broad as the figures.

A month or two later I met Lord St. Aldwyn by what men call chance. After the usual greetings:

"Will you come my way?' he asked.

"It is the only way I can go now," he added smiling, "but I still walk as much as I can."

I hardly knew what to say: he looked his age; the immitigable years had done their work. "Black Michael" was an old, old man; the end in sight.

Suddenly our previous conversation and the memory of the land-sale came into my head together:: was that his "last fight?"

I felt uncomfortable. Did he notice my silence? I can not tell. I cannot tell how the talk began, nor how much of it was plain speech on his part or inference on mine. I can only give my impression. He began, I think about titles, asking me to omit the "handle" as before.

"You don't care for titles, do you? I don't think I do either, much—still I have a son, you know, Quenington. If I had had only my three gals, I'd never have asked the King for the title; though to tell truth he proposed it himself. In England it's part of the reward——"

I nodded my head: I could not speak: I had hoped so much more from the man who at the outset had fought Lord Clanricarde and all his own world to boot, for right's sake and justice.

I had always hoped and believed that wise men grew less selfish as the came near the end. Eyes unseeled, desires quenched, the soul-wings lifting . . . and now . . . it was too painful.

He went on impatiently.

"Reward! I could not live on my pay as Cabinet Minister: what's 5,000 pounds a year for a man with a country place to keep up and a town house besides? I was a poor baronet, an intolerable position . . . poverty is a bad counselor . . . in a member of the governing classes idiotic. A temptation and worse . . . the public will gain through paying their real leaders properly. The house gives a second-rate general a title and 50,000 pounds to keep it up on (was he thinking of Kitchener?). Why shouldn't they give me money for over fifty years of work—a small reward, I call it . . . very small."

That, then, was the *Apologia!* It flashed through my mind that that was the soul of the man, that he was all of a piece, English, long-headed, practical in spite of his idealism, a real man in a real world, with strong paternal love probably for his son, and a great desire to do right, to act fairly, to justify himself if he had failed of the high mark. Most men become more selfish and not less as the grow old: it is only the poets and seers—the choice and master-spirits of the world—who turn sweeter with the years, and strong and true though Hicks-Beach was, he was not one of the Sacred Band. Yet, on the whole, and compared with other men, even with other men of genius like Lord Randolph Churchill, he was a *good* man, not a bad one, an honest man, too: at least as Hamlet said of himself, "indifferent honest!" as honest as the evil times permitted. I was glad I could reconcile my faith with my deep liking for the person.

"I agree with you," I said when he had finished. "The laborer is worthy of his hire. I have known no better laborer than you in England, but many who demanded and took a much greater reward."

"I felt sure you would understand," he said: "the few do, and the others don't matter. I'm glad to have had this talk.

"I wish you'd come down to Coln St. Aldwyn and stop a week this summer. The place looks so much better in summer: you'd know then how a man comes to love it. I'm always glad to get back home." I excused myself after thanking him, and we parted.

I stood and looked after him.

"One of the ablest and certainly the most honest English statesmen of my time," I said to myself.

\* \* \* \* \* \* \*

In the last week of April 1915 came the news that his son, Lord Quenington, had been killed at the front in France, leaving, however, a young son to inherit the place and title. A week later the great Earl gave up, too, and full of years (he was over eighty) was gathered to his fathers in the old house he loved so well. The park and the gardens rise before me as I write: the English wild flowers on the borders five yards deep are swaying and curtsying in the sun and warm southwest wind while the chestnut trees are holding ivory lamps against the green.

Augustus John

# AUGUSTUS JOHN

IT was Montaigne who said that height was the only beauty of man, and indeed height is the only thing that gives presence to a man. A miniature Venus may be more attractive than her taller sisters, but a man must have height to be imposing in appearance or indeed impressive.

Of all the men I have met Augustus John has the most striking personality. Over six feet in height, spare and square shouldered, a good walker who always keeps himself fit and carries himself with an air, John would draw the eye in any crowd. He is splendidly handsome with excellent features, great violet eyes and long lashes. Were it not for a certain abruptness of manner he would be almost too good-looking; as it is, he is physically, perhaps, the handsomest specimen of the genus homo that I have ever met.

And John has the great manner to boot. I remember one night at dinner he threw back his head in flagrant disagreement with something said, and quoted Rossetti's famous translation of the Villon verses: "Where Are the Snows of Yesteryear," with a pasionate enthusiasm that swept aside argument and infected all his hearers. Every one felt in the imperious manner, flaming eyes and eloquent cadenced voice the outward and visible signs of that demonic spiritual endowment we call genius.

John has had a curious history. He went to the Slade School of Design in London as a boy and studied there for some years. He was a quiet, studious youth, rather solitary in his habits, in no way remarkable or even conspicuous. One summer holiday, however, a friend tells me, he went to the Welsh coast for the sea-bathing. He dived in one day and struck his head on a rock. His companions pulled him out and carried him home. He was put to bed and the doctor declared that his patient must be kept quiet; he was probably suffering from concussion of the brain.

In a few months, however, John got all right again and went back to London and school, where for the first week he wore a skull cap. But to the astonishment of my informant he was a new John; a John who was curiously arrogant and contemptuous even of the great masters. He surprised everybody at once by his wonderful power of drawing and his weird and defiant looseness of living. The friend who tells me the story declares that John owes his genius to that blow on the head. I give the tale for what it is worth, because it corresponds loosely to the fact that John came into possession of his astonishing talent for drawing and his habit of unconventional living with surprising abruptness.

I came to know John pretty well in London and was at once an enthusiastic admirer of his drawing if not of his painting. He was, and is, a draughtsman of the first rank, to be compared with Ingres, Durer and Degas, one of the great masters, but the quality of his painting is poor—gloomy and harsh—reflecting, I think a certain disdainful bitterness of character which does not go with the highest genius.

John stayed with me once for two or three days in the south of France. He was an extraordinary interesting companion. He had just been through the north of Italy, had studied at Orvieto the mosaics and frescos of Signorelli, and been enormously impressed by them. He talked enthusiastically of the master's brains and powers; he would place him, he declared, above Michaelangelo and Leonardo, a supreme artist.

I was the more inclined to listen to him, because he showed himself on occasion a very good judge of literature, with a curious liking for what I would call the abnormalities of real life, which he found infinitely more suggestive and more inspiring than any artistic conventions. He was well-read in modern English verse, but had a particular passion for the Romany tongue and the vagrant gypsy people.

"Whatever is out of the common appeals to me", he said, "and here you have a nation of nomads who acknowledge no canons of civilized life and yet manage as pariahs if not as outlaws to exist and propagate their kind. I not only respect and admire their fanatic independence, but I enjoy talking to them and living with them. I have tried it in Wales and found them far more sympathetic and companionable than my own race, and I have tried it in France just as successfully, perhaps, because the gypsy women are frankly sensuous and their men prefer stealing to huckstering. Besides they haven't a touch of religious hypocrisy, and that's what I most detest."

John is a rebel at heart, perhaps, even more of a rebel than I am. He praised some of my stories beyond measure, so that I gave him the first sketch of my book on Oscar Wilde, but he did not like my pointing out to Wilde that his peculiarity was vicious, he himself a sort of arrested development. He would have it that Wilde had as much right to his tastes and their gratification as any man. "Pheasant or partridge," John declared cynically, "who shall decide; let every man eat what he prefers."

"Even human flesh?" I queried.

"Why not," replied John defiantly; "if it came my way and pleased me, I should eat it."

His view of life is that of the realist-skeptic. He regards all belief in progress and improvement as a superstition. What is, is all we have and there is no use in grumbling or kicking. After all, this world is a pretty good place for the healthy and fortunate. Live your life to the full is the whole duty of man, according to John. He would accept Shakespeare's phrase in Lear, "Ripeness is all"; but still the idea of perfection commands the homage of the sincere and rules conduct.

Ten years ago as to-day John was a law unto himself and lived outside all English conventions and English social life in spite of the fact that many great ladies and some men would willingly have made a lion of him.

Sir Hugh Lane, the Irish art critic, was one of his earliest admirers. He went down, it will be remembered, in the Lusitania. After he had made his money Sir Hugh took a house in Chelsea and determined to get Augustus John to execute some frescoes in the hall and dining-room. John, it is said, got a large sum down and immediately went to work, first prudently stretching canvas over the walls so that his work might not be exposed to the inclemencies of weather. He had sketched in several nudes from the life when one day a lady came in, Lady Lane, I think, and was dreadfully shocked. She insisted that John should stop. He packed up his material and left Lane to finish the picture himself, if he cared to. I saw his work and thought it superb; no greater master of line has lived.

During the war he was made a major in the Canadian army. The farewell party he gave in Chelsea is still talked of as the wildest orgy London had seen for many a year. Twelve or fifteen painters and writers sat up all night drinking, and when in the morning the Staff car came to the door for John, the tipsy guests gave him a great send off. When he arrived at Boulogne it is said he was still drunk and became disorderly when he was reprimanded for having his spurs on upside down. He would wear the damned things, he declared, as he pleased. After some months a letter came to the War Office from his commanding officer declaring that Major John had imbibed enough atmosphere and whiskey to paint the whole of France—red.

On his return to England he soon showed that he had not altered, for he was nearly court-martialed for knocking down a superior officer who contradicted him at a social gathering at the Duke of Manchester's. John is regarded as frankly impossible in society in spite of his good looks and splendid talent. To me the rebel is always infinitely more interesting than the conventional gentleman. I cannot help believing that the rebel gives more to humanity than the conventional person, because he learns more and because of the something dæmonic in him which alone could induce him to revolt in England, the home of convention. Yet I do not believe it helps to kick against the pricks too often or too hard.

The question remains, what has John given to the world? A good critic the other day assured me that John was the first living English painter; that his great cartoon forty feet long and fifteen feet high of the Canadians opposite Lens in the winter of 1917-18 is one of the great cartoons of the world, worthy to be compared with those of Michelangelo and Leonardo. I do not agree with this estimate: it seemes too quiet far too orderly to represent gassed and choking troops. Yet from the reproduction of it that I have seen it appears to me to be fine— —John at his best. The scene depicts Canadian troops, stretcher bearers and German prisoners, while on the left French women and children are flying from the scene; in the background a shell bursting and between it and a flare of light a great figure of the Christ, evidently a sort of village shrine. A profoundly interesting cartoon that may well be of high value.

But John's pictures, as I have said, fail to satisfy me in spite of the really magnificent quality in them.

I remember a picture called "The Orange Jacket" in

which a gypsy woman's face and figure are set forth with astonishing vividness; the black head; the hair all over her forehead matching her black eyes; the thick lips and intentness of the gaze balanced by the orange-red of the jacket and the white and blue of the blouse. But I prefer a picture called "The Red Handkerchief." A girl's figure with wind-tossed hair. I remember still the shadowy eyes and the blue dress set off by a red handkerchief carried in the right hand. The figure is superbly rendered; very summarily, yet the lissomeness given to the slight round form is arresting—splendidly sensual this with the spiritual note as well in the brooding mystery of the eyes.

"The Washing Day" comes before me as I write. A woman in a garden washing at a basin with her red shirt picked out with white and a red cap of the same material on her black hair; clothes of various colors are drying over the line in the distance, and each color from the green of the trees to the ochre of some piled-up brick is of value in a consummate composition.

Some of John's landscapes, too, are unforgetable; a little lake in the mountains; the heathy foreground just indicated while the sky's worked out in realistic detail of an astounding beauty and the whole synthetised into an emotion of evening and haunting tranquil loveliness.

Finally I recall two gypsy girls in profile, half figures, draped in bright colors; both are finished minutely to every whorl even in the ears; perhaps, because they are not even pretty, there is over the whole a feeling of brooding, sullen, bestial sensuality, arresting yet suggestive as a personal confession.

And yet I am not content. I had hoped that John would be with Rembrandt and Velasquez—a new star in the firmament. But he is content, it seems, to be in the second line with men like Degas. Still, he is only about forty and may yet do greater work than any he has given us. He seems to have turned his head away from the modern school; he has gone half-way along the road with Cezanne, but not the whole way. I remember a picture of Gauguin even, a Tahitian Venus thrown naked on her face on a bed, that is at once more sensual and more finely conceived than anything John has done. And Cezanne has painted one or two heads of contemporaries with more astonishing mastery than anything John has shown. Yet with his prodigious talent he may still do wonders. I can only hope that he will yet fulfill the dreams of his youth. He would be inclined, I am afraid, to add cynically the French proverb, *Songes sont mensonges.*

In this sketch I seem to have laid stress on John's drinking. I have never seen him the worse for drink nor do I believe that that vice has any attraction for a man of his high intellect and imperious character. He would drink, I imagine, if at all, out of a sort of bravado and because he can no doubt by virtue of splendid health stand a good deal without showing any signs of it. But the legend about him in London is of drink and orgies, because he defies conventions, and drunkenness is the English symbol of all rebellion, whether moral or immoral, because the English have no conception of any revolt coming from above. The Jews, it will be remembered, in the same spirit, spoke of Jesus as being a winebibber and a sinner.

John's pitfall is not drink.

If John does not realize himself to the uttermost, doesn't mint all the gold in him, it will be, I am sure, because he has been too heavily handicapped by his extraordinary physical advantages. His fine presence and handsome face brought him to notoriety very speedily, and that's not good for a man. Women and girls by the dozen have made up to him and he has spent himself in living instead of doing his work. Art is the most absorbing of all mistresses and the most jealous: "You must feel more than any other man," she orders, "and yet remain faithful to the high purpose." *Many are called and few are chosen.*

Coventry Patmore

# COVENTRY PATMORE

*"This land of such dear souls, this dear, dear land,
Dear for her reputation through the world."*
—Shakespeare.

THIS is what England has always been to me, "the land of such dear souls." Her reputation through the world is not what Shakespeare thought it, thanks mainly to her politicians; but I have said enough about that elsewhere. Here I am only concerned to tell of the dear souls in England, and among them in my time none was dearer than Coventry Patmore, partly because of the extraordinary whimsies and peculiarities that set off his fine mind and noble generosity of character.

It seemed to surprise Englishmen even to see us together. Patmore as a high poet and Catholic protagonist was of the elect and select, for then as now the Catholic hierarchy and the Catholic nobility were the guardians so to say of Society's Holy of Holies, and that Patmore should be seen about with an American and Socialist journalist, appeared to the average Briton a desecration. When they found out that I admired and loved him and that he liked me and my work, they were still more astonished, for as a rule he held himself aloof from men with a singular dignity and used his position as poet and seer to speak his mind at all times with perfect sincerity and most un-English frankness.

His judgements were by no means infallible; always tinctured indeed by personal feeling, but they came from such an austere moral height that they always commanded respect in England and acquiescence if not acceptance.

I remember once the question of the hundred best books was brought up by Mr. Frederick Greenwood, the editor of the *St. James Gazette,* and Coventry Patmore astonished the table when he was appealed to, by the statement: "When I was in the British Museum I used to say there were forty miles of useless books; all the good literature of the world could be put in forty feet."

"Why The Fathers of the Church alone would fill that space," cried one who would be witty.

"Fathers of the Church indeed in the true sense," was Patmore's incisive retort.

There was a sort of gasp at the novelty of the thought and phrase, but I agreed with the judgement enthusiastically; in fact, I had always thought that four feet even would be sufficient; that all the memorable things in Shakespeare for instance would go in a dozen pages.

It surprised me to think of Coventry Patmore in the British Museum and so I asked him about it, and he told me quite unaffectedly a remarkable story. It appeared that his father had been very well off till he took a hand in the great railway gamble of 1845 and lost nearly everything. Coventry had just published his first book of poems at twenty-one and for a couple of years had to live by his pen. He always attributed his lung weakness and delicacy of constitution in later life to this period of privation, but I believe he exaggerated the matter; poverty and even long-continued hunger at twenty-one very seldom affect the constitution. But he resented the petty miseries and told me with keenest pleasure how a casual meeting with Mr. Monckton Milnes, afterwards, Lord Houghton, at Mrs. Procter's, had changed his whole outlook. A few days after the meeting he was astonished at receiving a letter from Milnes telling him to present himself at the British Museum where he would be accepted as one of the assistants, Mr. Milnes having already written to the Archbishop of Canterbury and other Trustees about him.

It seems that after dinner in the drawing-room, Milnes said to Mrs. Procter:

"Who is your lean young friend with the frayed coat cuffs?"

"You wouldn't talk in that way," the lady answered, "if you knew how clever he is and how unfortunate. Have you read his *Poems?*"

Milnes took them away in his pocket and wrote to her next morning: "If your young friend would like a post in the library of the British Museum, it shall be obtained for him, if only to induce you to forget what must have seemed my heartless flippancy. His book is the work of a true poet, and we must see that he never lacks butter for his bread."

Patmore told me incidentally that the "poems" which had won him this recognition were "trash, and not worth considering."

What other country is there where a man of Monckton Milnes' position would have thought it his duty to help a poverty-stricken young poet? Another "dear soul" was the man Carlyle christened "Dicky Milnes, the canary bird."

So in 1846 Patmore was appointed to a position which he declared of "all the world was the best suited to him." He kept his place for twenty years and then retired with the respect of everyone and the magnificent pension of six or seven hundred dollars a year, which was the largest the trustees could allot him.

Frederick Greenwood, I think it was, who introduced me to Coventry Patmore shortly before I took over the editorship of the *Fortnightly Review* in '87. Patmore at the time was sixty-three or sixty-four years of age. He must have been tall as a young man; he was still perhaps five feet ten or so, thin to emaciation, with an upright dignity of carriage and imperiousness of manner; his likings and dislikings already aphoristic as if he had thought much about the subjects and come to very definite and pointed conclusions. His forehead was curiously broad like Caesar's; his chin, large and bony; his eyes, too, gray, keen, challenging; altogether he looked like a man of action rather than a poet.

The extravagant contradictions in him appealed to me intensely. At a dinner at the Grosvenor Hotel once with Greenwood he showed himself a more extreme Tory than Greenwood. At one moment he referred to the poem in which he called the enfranchisement of the working class "the great crime"; the next he declared that Gladstone would assuredly be damned for his "oklocratic sentimentalities". He is known to have written the famous parody of the triumphant telegram which Kaiser Wilhelm sent to his wife after the victory of Woerth in 1870:

"This is to say, my dear Augusta,
We've had another awful buster.
Ten thousand Frenchmen sent below,
Praise God from whom all blessings flow."

Patmore cared nothing for the social uplift of the working class; "no spiritual improvement in it," he opined; he would not see that some material betterment had to come before any spiritual growth was possible. He preached the gospel of peace and love, yet at the same time insisted upon an increase of militarism; got into a fever about the smallness of the British navy, and saw the hope of the world in British domination.

With a spice of malevolence I quoted to him Emerson's last speech before leaving England: "If the heart of England fail in the chances of a commercial crisis, I shall look to the future of humanity westward of the Alleghany Mountains."

In spite of his youthful admiration for Emerson, Patmore shrugged his shoulders and barked derisively; "and the future of poetry I suppose in Walt Whitman."

I took up the challenge instantly. "You might do worse," I said, "some of Walt Whitman can be read side by side with the last chapter of Ecclesiastes."

"I'd like to hear that," he scoffed. So I recited some verses to him and at once he grew thoughtful and at length admitted reluctantly: "That's fine; I hadn't seen it; but most of his stuff is drivel; no power of self-criticism in him—the hall-mark and obverse of creative genius. Poe is the only singer America has produced, and even he—"

Patmore was a most excellent host and after the meal gave us a bottle of Comet port, which Greenwood plainly relished.

"Tennyson's tipple," I remarked.

"You pay my wine a poor compliment," answered Patmore, laughing. "Tennyson used to send for his port to the nearest pub; it was quantity and not quality he wanted; strength, not bouquet."

"Do you admire his work?" I asked; "nearly all his later stuff bores me; after thirty he had nothing new in his pouch."

"Patmore," interrupted Greenwood, "was the man who found the true word for it. He called the early poetry Tennyson and the latter poetry Tennysonian." One could not but laugh.

A little while after this I got a letter from Patmore asking me to remember my promise to come down to stay with him at Hastings. I went down for a weekend and never enjoyed a couple of days more in my life.

Eager to get the heart of his mystery, pondering how best to extract a confession of his beliefs and hopes, I was taken aback by his house, which was really the finest house in Hastings, with a dozen or more bedrooms and a superb drawing-room and a cozy study in front. From his work in the British Museum I had expected modest comfort and *res angusta domi,* but found wealth and a mansion set in three or four acres of ground which had been converted into an old Italian garden with country house terraces and forest trees, all in the middle of a busy watering place and almost on the old London road. A proper dwelling for a poet, but how did Patmore get the money to keep up this large and luxurious life?

As unaffectedly as he had told about his poverty he told of his misery after the death of his first wife, "The Angel in the House," a wretched loneliness which ended in coughing and weakness and drove him for a long winter to the Riviera and Rome. Rome, which made Luther a Protestant made Coventry Patmore a Catholic. There he met his second wife, a religious devotee, proposed to her and was accepted, then found out that she was rich, which shocked him so that for a time he questioned the advisability of marriage; did not think he was good enough. But in the long run he married her and enjoyed fourteen years of almost perfect happiness.

Curiously enough he made no secret of the fact that he had loved his first wife better. "I made a half-joke to Mary about it once," he said. "I wrote her:

"I could not love thee, dear, so *much*,
Loved I not Honor more."

Honor was the name he gave his first wife, Emily, in his poem *The Angel in the House*. When I went to bed that night with this confession in my ears I threw myself on the bed and laughed till I ached. It never even occured to the poet that Mary might resent the secondary place, and indeed it seems never to have occurred to her, a fact which convinced me that my knowledge of women and their power of self-abnegation was worse than inadequate.

"For dear to maidens are their rivals dead," Patmore writes in *Amelia* with a sublime absence of humor.

His second wife was forty-two when she married; the bond between these two seems to have been more spiritual than is usually the case. Mary had no children of her own apparently contented herself with playing foster-mother to her husband's household. By all accounts she was peculiarly shy and timid.

Patmore had the originality of a fine mind developed in solitude; he loved convivality and men's talk occasionally; but had always lived with his own thoughts, and like the monarch his words were stamped with his own image and superscription.

On my first visit we spent the whole day together and found various points where our minds touched. He was delighted that I liked Pascal; but to my wonder praised him not for loftiness of thought as much as for his hatred of Jesuit priests.

"I knew we should get along together," he chirped, "as soon as I heard you tell Greenwood that you hated Manning and loved Newman; the one's a self-seeking priest, the other a spiritual guide and apostle."

Emerson, he confessed, had led him to Swedenborg; but when I mentioned Garth Wilkinson and Emerson's praise of him, he surprised me by lifting his eyebrow's and shrugging his shoulders in contempt.

"Swedenborg," he persisted, "is inspired, plainly inspired."

I pressed him about Boehme, but he had not read him, and so I was again at a loss and could at first get no clear light on his mystical faith.

But on a later visit he talked to me enthusiastically of the Spaniard St. John of the Cross and from the Spaniard's sensual ecstasies I began to get glimpses of Patmore's real belief. To my astonishment he was a mystic in only one point. His love for his first wife was so passionate, so overwhelming, that it became an inspiration to him, so much so that when on the point of going over to Rome he hesitated; how could he reconcile the faith and fervor of "The Angel in the House" with Catholic doctrine? With ingenuous casuistry it was suggested to him that such ecstatic love was the very soul of the Catholic religion and at once all his difficulties disappeared. Ever afterward he talked like the Biblical commentators of the desire of the soul for the Church, as the desire of the woman for the man by whom she reaches fruition, and more than once he told me that this was the theme of his greatest and most mature work, the *Sponsa Dei*, which he had worked at for five or six years.

Some time later in his study he said he had burned this prose book, his finest work, because it might have become a stumbling block to weaker brethren: Father Gerard Hopkins, an extraordinary half-genius, had thought some passages lent themselves to misconstruction, as indeed they did, and he had, therefore, burned the manuscript.

That evening after dinner Patmore's mood grew more and more confiding and intimate. I found he admired

Schopenhauer almost as much as I did, and this led me again to question his mysticism.

"Your mind and mine," he explained, "are antipodes one of the other, and therefore really in close relation. For example, you shocked me yesterday by talking of the Song of Solomon in the Bible as a mere love song; a hymn of passion you called it. I always think of the relation between husband and wife as the relation of the soul to Christ, an intimacy of supernal joy, of highest inspiration; I regard this merging of one's self in a supreme unity as the passionate symbol of the love of the soul for God. This to me is the truth of truths, the burning heart of the universe."

He said this with a sort of mystical rapture, gripping the arms of the chair and chanting out the words with quivering voice and intense feeling. . . . A moment later he began again as if to justify himself; "all women to me when unspoiled by men are wonderfully good, angels that make the home, and I look forward to reunion with absolute certitude. If I told you, if I could tell you, that she has come to me often with heavenly counsels of grace——" he got up and moved about the room and finally took a cigarette and relapsed into a silence broken only by an occasional sigh.

This then was the heart of him, his secret, so to speak. The phrase of Tertullian has been used about him—*"Mens naturaliter Catholica";* but I would qualify this by saying that it was love for a women led him to love of the Divine—as he said himself: "Love that grows from one to all."

"Love is my sin," cries Shapespeare; but love was Patmore's religion, the faith by which he lived and died, and no one has sung the delirious idealization of first love with such impassioned ecstasy:

> "His merits in her presence grow
> To match the promise in her eyes,
> And round her happy footsteps blow
> The authentic airs of Paradise."

Or take his mysticism in prose:

"The obligatory dogmata of the Church are only the seeds of life. The splendid flowers and the delicious fruits are all in the corollaries, which few, besides the saints, pay any attention to. Heaven becomes very intelligible and attractive when it is discovered to be—Woman.

A Mohammedan would have applauded his creed!

Patmore, I felt, was always too insubordinate to be a representative Catholic; yet by virtue of a fine mind and passionate devotion he stands with Cardinal Newman in the great English Catholic revival of the nineteenth century, much as Dante stood six centuries earlier, called and chosen "to justify the ways of God to men." Little by little I became aware of the fragrance of his nature like an incense rising ever in gratitude and love to Him who had made his paths the paths of peace.

I wonder when I say Catholic mystic if I can get my readers to understand at all the profound joyful piety of the man. There was no high poetry but what was religious to him. He would have no work of art that did not concern itself chiefly with God and man. He saw my story "Montes" in the *Fortnightly Review* and wrote me a flaming condemnation of it. The execution was almost perfect, he said, but the matter was horrible. I answered him by pointing out that my theme was much the same as that of Othello. He accepted this at once, but stuck to his verdict. No authority, not even that of Shakespeare, could induce him even to modify his judgment. I give it here; in his own words; for I regard it as intensely characteristic:

Dear Mr. Harris:

The manner, the technical element, in your three papers seems to me to be beyond criticism. The severity with which you confine yourself to saying things, instead of talking about them, is wholly admirable. My criticism must be about the matter.

The "Matador" as a piece of mere representation could scarcely be improved upon. The matter too, is novel and striking. But I am of the very small minority who will be disposed to complain that it wants what is most essential in art, a properly human interest. The hero is a wild beast, the heroine a bitch.

Another page of the same letter gives his views on my *Modern Idyll*, the story of a Western Minister's love for his deacon's wife. Patmore's condemnation is passionate enough to prove that I have not underrated his religious fervor or overpraised his power of expression. He says that *A Modern Idyll* is probably characteristic of America and shows there "a state of things compared with which Dante's and Swedenborg's hells are pleasant to contemplate. Yet I doubt, nay, more then doubt, whether this actual hell, this putrid pool irrisdescent, with the cant of pietism and steaming with profanation of divine names and ideas, is not too horrible to be exposed as you have exposed it.

For hours after reading it, I felt shocked and sickened as I do not remember to have been by any other writing; and I cannot think that anything but evil can come to the ordinary reader of it.

Kipling never did anything better than the "Triptych"; that is to say, the kind of thing which was thought worth doing could not have been done better.

Of course Kipling with his Tory Imperialism appealed to Patmore intensely; when one objected to his shallow cleverness and cocksureness Patmore replied: "To paint this age of ours he had to use vulgarity as a pigment."

Patmore's point of view interested me immensely, for it is the attitude of latter-day Christianity. They clothe the statues in St. Peter's with tin just as the ladies in Chicago are supposed to clothe the piano legs in pyjamas. And the Bishops of the Anglican Church agree with the Catholic Cardinals that sins of the flesh are chiefly to be reprobated.

"Tigers devouring a deer may be a subject for art," Patmore argued, "but not for great art. . . . The passions, desires and appetites which men share with the brute creation are not a fitting subject for supreme presentation; it is only the things that are purely human, or if you will, divine, that make high art possible."

"There are long-calculated revenges," I objected,

"meannesses and envyings, too, that are purely human, yet viler than the beasts."

But he wouldn't have it. The human part of man was all good—one with the divine.

And just as he cared nothing for the social struggle of our age, so he cared little for the star-sown field of space. In one poem in *The Unknown Eros*, his finest work, he has put the two beliefs side by side:
"Put by the Telescope!
Better without it man may see,
Stretch'd awful in the hush'd midnight,
The ghost of his eternity."

Fancy a sane man writing those three words, "better without it!" Yet the passionate fervor of the next three lines explain if they cannot justify the absurdity.

I got to love Patmore. An optimist in everything that concerned himself and his private life, a pessimist with regard to others and to politics; perfect faith in a Heaven of eternal bliss, absolute disbelief in any progress in the world or even improvement, he would inveigh for hours against what he called the "rot" of the daily press and the vile lies it disseminates and then tell a joke against himself with the hugest delight. Nor was he ever prudish or mealy mouthed; he left "prudery to the Puritan half-believers," he said, scornfully.

Patmore was grateful by nature in all things as few men are. He told me how he had sought and obtained a very early copy of St. Thomas Aquinas in seventeen volumes on vellum, and had given the book to the British Museum.

"I owe so much to the Museum," he said simply, "I was glad to acknowledge my immense debt."

He had the highest artistic standard. "An imperfect line," he said, "lies on my conscience like a sin and I never rest until I have got it right, even if it costs me years."

And he lived up to this. Here is an ode of his, *Departure*, that I think is of supreme quality; it is evidently to his first wife, Emily, though written years after her death, and is drenched in love and pathetic as the slow heavy tears of age which always remind me of the drops of moisture that exude from stone:

## DEPARTURE.

"It was not like your great and gracious ways!
Do you, that have nought other to lament,
Never, my Love, repent
Of how, that July afternoon,
You went.
With sudden unintelligible phrase,
And frighten'd eye,
Uupon your journey of so many days,
Without a single kiss, or a good-bye?
I knew, indeed, that you were parting soon;
And so we sate, within the low sun's rays,
You whispering to me, for your voice was weak,
Your harrowing praise.
Well, it was well,
To hear you such things speak,
And I could tell
What made your eyes a growing gloom of love,
As a warm South-wind sombres a March grove.

And it was like your great and gracious ways
To turn your talk on daily things, my Dear,
Lifting the luminous, pathetic lash
To let the laughter flash,
Whilst I drew near,
Because you spoke so low that I could scarcely hear.
But all at once to leave me at the last,
More at the wonder than the loss aghast,
With huddled, unintelligible phrase
And frighten'd eye,
Upon your journey of all days
With not one kiss, or a good-bye,
And the only loveless look the look with which you pass'd;
'Twas all unlike your great and gracious ways.

Yet fine as Patmore's best work is and of a magnificent and austere simplicity, it is seldom sensuous and passionate enough to belong to the highest poetry. He never comes near the best of Goethe or Keats or Shakespeare. His simplicity often degenerates into triviality; his sentiment is often mawkish. Some one said of him once wittily: "Patmore never realizes the sublime in others, or the ridiculous in himself."

Just as some of us think we have outlived Catholicism, so we have certainly outlived Patmore's literary judgments. He never dreamed of a synthesis of Paganism and Christianity, of the reconciliation of body and soul, and so the best of our modern insight was beyond him. He liked Carlyle because "he and I are the only two who dare to dislike and despise Heine," and at the same time dismissed "Carlyle, Ruskin and Thackeray as second-rate minds"; indeed, he seemed to place Ruskin above Carlyle, which to me was worse than blasphemy.

With many of Patmore's literary opinions I was in cordial agreement. I, too, loved Coleridge and Keats, and thought little of Shelley and Clough and other gods of popular idolatry. Rossetti, however, I esteemed more highly than Patmore, who scoffed at his scanty knowledge of English literature and summed him up by declaring he was "tense and not intense"—an epigrammatic misstatement. In talk he often raged against Rossetti as a sort of anti-Christ, though they had once been friends and Rossetti was one of the first openly to praise Patmore's poetry.

But Patmore was often finely right, as when he declared that Tennyson's best work, though a miracle of grace, was never quite "the highest kind"; and he explained this unconsciously by recording the fact that "his (Tennyson's) incessant dwellings upon trifles concerning himself, generally small injuries, real or imaginary, was childish." Browning he underrated and Blake, too, as much as he overprized Mrs. Meynell, whom he seriously proposed for Poet Laureate.

Coventry Patmore though always masterful, often arbitrary and prone to contradict, was a staunch friend, a kind and generous host: and above all, a prince of companions to a man of letters, a very interesting poet, a noble husband and father. He represented to me all that was best in English life, and if he showed the religious spirit in wild exaggeration, that too is English and intensely characteristic.

To American readers I must prove that my praise of his poetry and natural piety is justified, so I give here his poem *The Toys* because of its universal appeal:

### THE TOYS.

"My little Son, who look'd from thoughtful eyes
And moved and spoke in quiet grown-up wise,
Having my law the seventh time disobey'd,
I struck him, and dismiss'd
With hard words and unkiss'd,
His Mother, who was patient, being dead.
Then, fearing lest his grief should hinder sleep,
I visited his bed,
But found him slumbering deep,
With darken'd eyelids, and their lashes yet
From his late sobbing wet.
And I, with moan,
Kissing away his tears, left others of my own;
For, on a table drawn beside his head,
He had put, within his reach,
A box of counters and a red-veined stone,
A piece of glass abraded by the beach
And six or seven shells,
A bottle with bluebells
And two French copper coins, ranged there with
    careful art,
To comfort his sad heart.
So when that night I pray'd
To God I wept, and said:
Ah, when at last we lie with tranced breath,

Not vexing Thee in death,
And Thou rememberest of what toys
We made our joys,
How weakly understood,
Thy great commanded good,
Then, fatherly not less
Than I whom Thou hast moulded from the clay,
Thou'lt leave Thy wrath, and say,
'I will be sorry for their childishness.' "

No wonder he was confident in his own pride of place:—many have been complacently sure of the laurel wreath with less reason. He wrote in 1886 as a preface to his complete works:

"I have written little, but it is all my best; I have never spoken when I had nothing to say, nor spared time or labor to make my words true. I have respected posterity, and, should there be a posterity which cares for letters, I dare hope that it will respect me."

Before I met him Patmore had married for the third time, and at sixty tasted "the full delight," as he said, for the first time of being a father. He was too busy, too full or care and too preoccupied with love to feel the relation very keenly with his first brood; but now he was fond to folly and delighted to repeat words of the boy-child, which were anything but remarkable. Patmore's ducks had always been swans. He even includes some of his eldest son's poetry with his own and used to insist that it was of the highest quality.

In this sketch I seem to have emphasized too much

Patmore's aristocratic attitude and beliefs; I should have added that he regarded the servants in his own house like his children and was not only kind but generous in his solicitude for the poor. After a storm once at Hastings that wrecked some of the poorer dwellings, he gave with both hands "to put the outcasts on their feet again," as he expressed it. And this he regarded as a simple duty; "we are all of the household of God," was his phrase.

And so he lived and died; on the surface a mass of contradictions because at odds with his time, but in spirit of a singular integrity; an aristocrat by nature and conviction in a growing, all-invading democracy; a lover and Catholic mystic in a sordid, scientific age; an Englishman who might have respected a Rabindranath Tagore, but would certainly have avoided friendly intercourse with him; an Englishman, I repeat, full of whimsies; a ferocious individualist born out of due season, yet lovable and beloved by his own even to reverence.

Walt Whitman

## WALT WHITMAN

IS THERE any relation I wonder between the size of a land and the greatness of the men born in it?
It seems to me sometimes as if the small countries produced the big men and great countries nothing but mediocrities. Rome, for instance, never produced any man at all commensurate with her grandeur; Athens and Jerusalem on the other hand gave birth to the greatest of men.

Reflecting in this way it occurred to me that if our globe were ten times as large as it is, we men would have to be mere pigmies; for if we were of our present stature we should be glued to the ground by the force of gravitation and unable to advance at all even by steps which are after all nothing but a series of fallings. On the other hand, if our world were only a tenth part of its present size, we men would have to be much larger in order that gravitation might keep us from skipping out of the world's pull altogether.

And so there may be some subtle and hitherto unexplained connection between small countries and great men and great countries and little men; but I soon reassured myself; the relation can hardly be inexorable, for America has produced three or four great men—Poe, Lincoln, Emerson and Walt Whitman.

Or do I now deceive myself? I think not. Whitman was so healthy and above all so well-proportioned that he perhaps seems smaller than he was. At any rate, this one can say with certainty, he is so far the most characteristic American and therefore also the most original.

But many Americans, Lowell among them, thought Lincoln "the first American," and Whitman himself praised him enthusiastically. How are we to decide whether Lincoln or Whitman was the greater? What is the criterion? Whitman supplies us with the measuring rod and, strange to say, it is also Goethe's, and historically approved I verily believe. Whitman writes: "Strange as it may seem the topmost proof of the race is its own born poetry . . . . the stamp of entire and finished greatness to any nation must be withheld till it has put what it stands for in the blossom of original first-class poems." Goethe goes even further and of course puts the idea much better:

"I have often said and will often repeat that the final cause and consummation of all natural and human activity is dramatic poetry."

It may be objected that these are two writers agreeing that poetry is the highest product of civilized man, but men of action might contradict them.

History, however, sustains the literary view. Carthage was rich and prosperous; Carthage disappeared and left no trace. Rome was mistress of the world for centuries; her language became the language of all civilized peoples. Rome fell and her place in our esteem and in our thoughts bcomes smaller and smaller as time goes on, whereas the place of Athens and Jerusalem becomes bigger and bigger and already the position of Jerusalem is higher than that of Rome or even of America because her poets and prophets were greater and are still a living force. Whoever then in America has produced the greatest poetry is the greatest man. I believe I am justified, therefore, in claiming pre-eminence for Whitman.

There is an amusing little side-light on Whitman to be won there. Scarcely has he established the fact to his own satisfaction that the highest purpose of civilization is the production of noble poetry when he goes on to talk of Scott and Tennyson, who, like Shakespeare, exhale that principle of caste which "we Americans have come on earth to destroy." Not to produce high poetry then but to destroy the spirit of caste is the great purpose of America. At his inspired moments Whitman knew better; again and again in his prose he recurs to the reverence we owe great men, to the benefit we all receive from that sacred admiration. If by the spirit of caste Whitman meant the adoration of wealth, or birth, or manners, or dress, or all of these, then indeed we may be said to have come here to destroy, but the false gods are only dethroned in the interests of the true god, and Whitman and Goethe are certainly justified in insisting that the poet and prophet will be more and more highly esteemed as man moves up the spiral of growth.

Great men are good companions, exhilarating and delightful as morning sunshine; their shortcomings even predict the future, for all imperfections forecast fulfilment and our faults pre-figure better men yet to be born.

But great men are a little difficult to know; even their lovers, to whom they give themselves freely, only come to understanding little by little. They are of infinite diversity; they say with Whitman—

> Do I contradict myself?
> Very well then I contradict myself;
> (I am large, I contain multitudes).

They are strange, too, and defy classification; at one moment the son of Man, at another the son of God; they are mysterious, ever conscious that they are a mystery, even to themselves, as indeed we all are.

But as a rule in youth they smack of the soil and betray the school, show us their beginnings and growth; the books they read and did not read. If you know the language they use and their time and condition, you have the key to them.

This man Whitman has few obvious marks of the school or of reading or of condition; he abjures all signs of servitude.

"You shall no longer take things at second or third hand, nor look through the eyes of the dead, nor feed on the spectres of books.

"You shall not look through my eyes either, nor take things from me.

"You shall listen to all sides and filter them from yourself."

## WALT WHITMAN 215

He asserts himself loudly:

"Clear and sweet is my soul. . . . .
Welcome is every organ and attribute of me and of any man healthy and clean."

Whitman is a pure man and as strange as the new continent where he was born. He is large like his land and rich in many ways, but incult for the most part and undeveloped, a great uncut gem with one small facet polished perfectly as if to show the supernal radiance of it.

For many years this strangeness, this want of cultivation, this untamed exuberance, the waste and wildness as of desert and mountain range, put me off; I regarded Emerson as the greatest American; but Emerson was bookish and a Puritan, and as I grew older I came to think more of the body and its claims and pleasures and Emerson's thin-blooded judgments became ridiculous to me. The French proverb *"bon animal bon homme"* imposed itself and the English prudery and conventionalism in Emerson distressed me as something worse than provincial. as a positive deformity, and I turned with delight to Whitman's broad humanity:

"I am the poet of the body and I am the poet of the
    Soul. . . . .
Walt Whitman, a kosmos, of Manhattan the Son,
Turbulent, fleshy, sensual, eating, drinking and breeding.
No sentimentalist, no stander above men and women or
    apart from them,
No more modest than immodest.

. . . . . . . . . .

Without shame the man I like knows and avows the
   deliciousness of his sex,
Without shame the woman I like knows and avows hers."

I began to do these penportraits with the fixed resolve only to write of men and women of importance whom I had known personally, and never to forget that one touch of soul-revealing drawn from intimate personal knowledge was worth pages of critical appreciation. The future will do its own criticising and its own appreciating; but generations still unborn must be grateful for just that personal knowledge of the "Shining Ones" which only those who knew them in the flesh, can supply.

Now I never knew Whitman: I mean by that, I saw him in passing, heard him speak—in Philadelphia in the winter of 1876 I believe it was; but hardly got from him more than an "Ay, Ay" to acknowledge understanding; yet an impression of the simplicity of the man remains with me and of his sanity and healthfulness.

He came on the platform slowly as if since his stroke he found walking a little difficult; he showed his age, too, in greying beard and hair; but his eyes were fine—steadfast, clear—and he had a certain air with him, the effect of goodly height, strong erect figure and greatness of nature. He certainly owed nothing to dress for his unstarched shirt was open at the neck, his waistcoat persisted in rucking up and his short-coat stuck out behind, making me smile at his likeness to a large Cochin fowl. But the whole impression was dignified, imposing; his voice was clear, his utterance deliberate, slow; his choice of words seemed to me good; a big man thoughtful, clear of eve and human, friendly to all.

Even this outline-sketch may be colored a little by later knowledge won from reading. However, I give it for what it is worth; having seen him in the flesh and heard his voice help me to realize him, and his large, untutored manhood.

In the same early poems, I have already used, Whitman makes his full confession in two lines:

"I believe in the flesh and the appetites,
Seeing, hearing, feeling are miracles and each part and
    tag of me is a miracle."

This might have been written by Goethe. Here for the first time we meet an Anglo-Saxon who has cut himself free from Puritanism and prudery without denying the mysteries.

In the fall of '81 shortly before Emerson's death, Whitman recalls the fact that "twenty-one years before on a bright sharp February midday I walked with Emerson, then in his prime, keen, physically and morally magnetic, armed at every point, and when he chose, wielding the emotional just as well as the intellectual. During those two hours he was the talker and I the listener. It was an argument, reconnoitering, review, attack, and pressing home (like an army corps in order, artillery, cavalry, infantry), of all that could be said against that part (and a main part) in the construction of my poems, "Children of Adam." More precious than gold to me that dissertation—it afforded me, ever after, this strange and paradoxical lesson; each point of Emerson's statement was unanswerable, no judge's charge ever more complete or convincing, I could never hear the points better put—and then I felt down in my soul the clear and unmistakable conviction to disobey all and pursue my own way.

" 'What have you to say to such things?' said E., pausing in conclusion. 'Only that while I can't answer them all, I feel more than ever to adhere to my own theory, and exemplify it," was my candid response.

"Whereupon we went and had a good dinner at the American House. And thenceforward I never wavered or was touched with qualms (as I confess I had been two or three times before)."

The poems under this heading "The Children of Adam," are all devoted to the sex-urge and have earned Whitman the reproach in his own country and in lesser degree in England, too, of being pornographic. From a French or Latin or Russian standpoint the poems are rather reticent and are indeed sadly to seek in several ways. But even an Anglo-Saxon before objecting to them might have considered the fact that they only fill fifteen pages out of over four hundred or less than four per cent. of the whole, which is surely a disproportionately small amount to be given in any full life to things sexual.

No wonder then that Emerson's arguments instead of convincing Whitman of wrongdoing filled him with the conviction that he had been right and removed all faintest doubts on the matter, or "qualms" as he calls them puritanically.

He sings "the body electric," and "a woman waits for me," and "the ache of amorous love," and yet I would call him ill-equipped on this side and uninteresting. He is frank, indeed, outspoken even, but astoundingly superficial—the heights and depths of passion have not been plumbed by him. Turn to "Solomon's Song," in the Bible and compare the two and you will find that the Jewish singer is infinitely Whitman's superior. Take the verses:

I sleep; but my heart waketh; it is the voice of my beloved that knocketh, saying open to me, my sister, my love, my dove, my undefiled, for my hair is wet with dew and my locks with drops of the night.

. . . . . . . . .

I don't need to quote a verse or two more in order to sound the deeps of desire; but let these two phrases from the heights be further witness:

"Thy lips are like a thread of scarlet" . . . and thy love "terrible as an army with banners."

The dread that always accompanies supreme passion was never more splendidly rendered. It makes everything in Whitman on this subject petty and slight. And this is the only real objection to be urged against "The Children of Adam" poems (an objection which Emerson surely never dreamed of), that they contain no new, great word on the matter, are in fact commonplace and as such unworthy of the eternal theme.

Think of the threnody of the Jewish song:

"Many waters cannot quench love; neither can the floods drown it; if a man would give all the substance

of his house for love, it would utterly be contemned...
And then the conclusion of the whole matter:
"For love is strong as death . . . jealousy is cruel as the grave."

It is not for their love-songs that the English and Americans are likely to be heard in the Court of Nations. And if they ever sought a hearing on this count they would do well to shoose Shakespeare or Swinburne (he wrote "In the Orchard" and "The Leper") to represent them rather than Whitman. But prudery in the United States has the malignity of an ague-fit and Americans shiver and burn with it alternately and are proud of its virulence, as children are proud of a physical deformity.

And accordingly Whitman fared ill at their hands, for many years after the publication of "The Leaves of Grass," till the day of his death indeed and long afterwards, his name was taboo in polite society, and in spite of his lofty democratic and religious utterances his book has never become popular in these States. Whitman's high position in the world of letters to-day has been given to him by foreign masters and he has been imposed on the American public by their eulogies, one more prophet *not without honor save in his own country and amid his own kin.*

Whitman himself testifies, without taint of bitterness, indeed with a noble unconcerned acceptance, to the completeness of the American boycott. Shortly before his death in the summer of his seventy-second year he wrote:

"All along from 1860 to '91, many of the pieces in

'Leaves of Grass' and its annexes, were first sent to publishers or magazine editors before being printed in the L. and were peremptorily rejected by them, and sent back to their author. The 'Eidolons' was sent back by Dr. H., of 'Scribner's Monthly' with a lengthy, very insulting and contemptuous letter. 'To the Sun-Set Breeze' was rejected by the editor of 'Harper's Monthly' as being 'an improvisation' only. 'On, On, Ye Jocund Twain' was rejected by the 'Century' editor as being personal merely. Several of the pieces went the rounds of all the monthlies, to be thus summarily rejected.

"June, '90. The———rejects and sends back my little poem, so I am now set out in the cold by every big magazine and publisher, and may as well understand and admit it—which is just as well, for I find I am palpably losing my sight and ratiocination."

And this ostracism is the more extraordinary because Whitman is a typical American in faults as in virtues. For example, he is perpetually praising "Democracy" and the "average" man; but when challenged on the matter he has to admit that the American democracy so far is a rank failure and the average man even in this blessed land leaves a great deal to be desired:

"For my part, I would alarm and caution even the political and business reader, and to the utmost extent, against the prevailing delusion that the establishment of free political institutions, and intellectual smartness, with general good order, physical plenty, industry, etc. (desirable and precious advantages as they all are) do, of themselves, determine and yield to our experiment of democracy the fruitage of success."

And though a little later he quotes Lincoln's famous apothegm "Government of the people, by the people, for the people," with high approval, in reality he is not blinded by words or sounding phrases; he writes:

"Genuine belief seems to have left us. The underlying principles of the States are not honestly believed in (for all this hectic glow and these melodramatic screamings) nor is humanity itself believed in. What penetrating eye does not everywhere see through the mask? The spectacle is appalling. We live in a atmospere of hypocrisy throughout. The men believe not in the women, nor the women in the men. A scornful superciliousness rules in literature."

And he sums up:

"I say that our New World democracy, however great a success in uplifting the masses out of their sloughs, in materialistic development products, and in a certain highly-decorative superficial popular intellectuality, is, so far, an almost complete failure in its social aspects, and in really grand religious, moral, literary and esthetic results. In vain do we march with unprecedented strides to empire so colossal, outvying the antique, beyond Alexander's, beyond the proudest sway of Rome. In vain have we annexed Texas, California, Alaska, and reach north for Canada and south for Cuba. It is as if we were somehow being endowed with a vast and more and more thoroughly-appointed body, and then left with little or no soul."

No wiser words of warning have yet been written in America.

Whitman is hypnotized by his love of "democracy" and the "average" man; yet he cannot but see that something is wrong with the formula and the creature.

"Will the time hasten," he cries, "when fatherhood and motherhood shall become a science—and the noblest science? To our model—the portrait of personality needed in these States—to our model a clear-blooded, strong-fibred physique is indispensable." He waits, too, "an erect attitude, a complexion showing the best blood, a voice whose sound outvies music; eyes of calm and steady gaze, yet capable also of flashing." Plainly Whitman's "average" man is a superman and his democracy a Utopia that in reach of imagination would shame Sir Thomas More's.

It might plausibly be argued that in spite of himself Whitman is an aristocrat from head to foot and demands physical, mental and moral perfection from all citizens.

On the other hand, it is only fair to admit that Whitman's passion for equality holds in itself a forecast of the future and its own justification. Who can doubt now in this marvellous year of 1919 that we are moving towards equality, destined gradually to realize it more and more in our institutions and in our lives, and with it the brotherhood of man. It seems to me significant that Whitman's poem "To Him That Was Crucified" as one brother and lover to another should be immediate-

ly followed by the verses to the "Felons on Trial in Courts" and prostitutes which ends in this way:
"Lusts and wickedness are acceptable to me,
I walk with delinquents with passionate love,
I feel I am of them—I belong to those convicts and prostitutes myself,
And henceforth I will not deny them—for how can I deny myself?"

In just this spirit Debs talked the other day on his trial: "As long as one man is in prison," he said, "I am in prison," and we all thrilled to the eternal truth.

Whitman's humanity, too, knows no exclusions:
"Not till the sun excludes you, do I exclude you."

He looks out upon "laborers, the poor and Negroes" with the same sense of kinship; he is human to the red heart of him and full of love; blood-brother to all men born. And this sense of universal sympathy and brotherhood is as fine as anything in him and does, as he saw, differentiate him as an American singer from all European singers as yet, conferring on him a singular distinction. But I cannot, alas, say even this much without lamenting in the same breath the fact that the majority of Americans of this time appear to have no inkling of their high calling, for they have been unable even to maintain the legal rights of free men handed down to them through half a dozen generations and protected explicitly by the Constitution. The torturing of conscientious objectors, too, in our prisons during the war, remains as an indelible stain on American civilazation.

Whitman, too, has his faults and in especial a shallow optimism which is peculiarly American; he says that "there are no liars or lies at all," but that "all is truth without exception," and all is health too, I presume, especially to those dying untimely of foul inherited diseases!

Again and again, too, his critical faculty betrays him. 'I can't imagine any better luck befalling these States for a poetical beginning and initiation than has come from Emerson, Longfellow, Bryant, and Whittier. Emerson to me stands unmistakably at the head, but for the others I am at a loss where to give any precedence. Each illustrious, each rounded, each distinctive . . . Longfellow . . . competing with the singers of Europe on their own ground and with one exception, better and finer work than any of them."

The exception, if you please, being Tennyson, as Whitman tells us elsewhere. Was there ever such criticism? The one, authentic, American poet, Poe, omitted altogether and Longfellow declared superior to Browning, Swinburne and Arnold in England, to Hugo, Verlaine and Sully Prudhomme in France, to Carducci in Italy; Longfellow, who is not worthy of being named with the least of these immortals. Bryant and Whittier too "illustrious and distinctive." It needed only one phrase to reach bathos and we get it: "Shakespeare as depicter of the passions is excelled by the best old Greeks as Aeschylus."

And with these blunderings I must set down also the dreadful neologisms which stain and disfigure most of his work such as, "promulge," "eclaircise," "deliveress," "partialist," "diminute," "ecleve," "acceptress" "exalte," "finale," "dolce," "affetuoso," "ostent," "inure," "effuse," "imperturbe," "buster," "Americanos," "rapport," and hundreds of similar blots upon the page.

Not one of these newcomers seems to have gained or deserved rights of naturalization in the language, and if one compares them to those coined by Coleridge, such as "atavism" and "atavistic," which do satisfy a need and enrich the common treasure-store, one will quickly realize the advantage of a thorough education.

Even when Whitman has a great theme and feels poignantly he perpetually hurts us with some word that is curiously inept and out of place. For instance, his dirge on Lincoln. "O Captain, my captain," has this line in it:

"For you bouquets and ribbon'd wreaths—for you the shores a-crowding."

How he could have written "bouquets" here without feeling the shock and incongruity, I can't imagine.

It seems to me that his love of so-called "free verse" springs from the same source; he not only resents bondage of any sort, but he is not highly articulate, not a master of his craft, a born singer. True, he has used free verse now and then most happily; but for each triumphant success how many comparative failures!

And both before and after him others have used freedom with happier results. Again and again in the Bible, for instance, as in the 13th chapter of Corinthians, and the last chapter of Ecclesiastes, and elsewhere prose has

## WALT WHITMAN

yielded as magical effects as have ever been attained by any poetry bond or free. Whitman's continual use of free verse has founded a school and, notably in America, has produced imitators who have not even studied the Biblical methods. There is no special virtue in rhythm; but nearly all the highest utterances in the world's literature have been musical, and free verse when it is unmusical is even more repulsive than halting or ill-sounding prose.

On this point I almost agree with Ruskin who wrote: "Irregular measure (introduced to my great regret in its chief wilfulness by Coleridge) is the calamity of modern poetry."

Of course one must remember that in talking of literature Whitman always takes the position that verbal excellence is of no moment, mere filigree and ornament; again and again he affirms that the deep purpose of his own poetry and indeed of all poetry is the religious purpose. He goes further here than even Emerson or Carlyle; he says:

"There can be no sane and complete personality, nor any grand and electric nationality without the stock (!) element of religion imbuing all the other elements . . . . so there can be no poetry worth the name without that element (religion) behind all."

But he is not content with vague generalities on this matter; "I am not sure," he says in the preface to the Centennial Edition of his works in 1876 when he was already 58 years of age: "I am not sure but the last inclosing sublimation of race or poem is what it thinks of death."

And he goes further:

"In my opinion it is no less than this idea of immortality, above all other ideas, that is to enter into and vivify and give crowning religious stamp of democracy in the New World."

And as if this were not enough he proceeds to tell us that "it was originally my intention after chanting in 'Leaves of Grass' the songs of the body and existence to compose a further and equally needed volume based on those convictions of perpetuity and conservation which . . . make the unseen soul govern absolutely at last."

"I mean to exhibit . . . the same ardent and fully appointed personality . . . with cheerful face, estimating death not at all as the cessation but as somehow what I feel it must be, the entrance upon by far the greatest part of existence and something that life is at least as much for as it is for itself.

.  .  .  .  .  .  .  .  .  .  .

"But the full construction of such a book is beyond my powers and must remain for some bard in the future.

.  .  .  .  .  .  .  .  .  .  .

"Meanwhile not entirely to give the go-by to my original plan. . . . I end my books with thoughts or radiations from thoughts on death, immortality and a free entrance into the spiritual world."

And in his famous "Passage to India," he cries:
"O daring joy but safe! are they not all the seas of God? O, farther, farther, farther sail!"

It is no vain boast of his that the "brawn of 'Leaves of Grass' is thoroughly spiritualized everywhere."

He is convinced of the necessity of this for "the Moral is the purport and lasting intelligence of all Nature." ... though "there is absolutely nothing of the moral in the works or laws of Nature."

And to make "full confession" he adds:

"I also sent out 'Leaves of Grass' to arouse and set flowing in men's and women's hearts, young and old, endless streams of living, pulsating love and friendship, directly from them to myself now and ever." He declares that this affection and sympathy will yet bring about the perfect union of all the States.

Thinking it all over, I feel that Whitman's unpopularity in America is almost as difficult to explain as Whistler's. When writing of Whistler I drew attention to the fact that his overwhelming love of beauty and his avoidance of anything coarse or mean, sordid or ugly, should have made him an immediate favorite in both England and America. It had not that effect, strange to say; and so when I think of Whitman's healthy animalism and the small space he gives it in his work and his passionate devotion to the implicit morality of things, to religion and even to immortality, I feel that he of all men should have been immediately popular in America; he is far and away the most characteristic product of this country; why did his countrymen decry his gospel and reject him? His purpose is their purpose, his belief their belief, his hope their hope!

Let us look at his best for a moment, for after all it is in his highest achievement even more than in his shortcomings that we discover the soul of a man.

The "Prayer of Columbus" is Whitman's best work; by much, I think, the noblest poem yet produced in these States. There is hardly a weak verse in the whole litany and there are lines in it of pure sublimity:
"O I am sure they really came from Thee
The urge, the ardor, the unconquerable will,
The potent, felt, interior command, stronger than words,
A message from the Heavens whispering to me even in sleep,
These sped me on.

. . . . . . . . . . . .

"The end I know not, it is all in Thee,
Or small or great I know not—haply what broad fields, what lands,
Haply the brutish measureless human undergrowth I know,
Transplanted there may rise to stature, knowledge worthy Thee,
Haply the swords I know may there indeed be turn'd to reaping-tools,
Haply the lifeless cross I know, Europe's dead cross, may bud and blossom there.

. . . . . . . . . . . .

One effort more, my altar this bleak sand;
That Thou O God, my life hast lighted,
With ray of light, steady, ineffable, vouchsafed of Thee,
Light rare untellable, lighting the very light,
Beyond all signs, descriptions, languages;
For that O God, be it my latest word, here on my knees,
Old, poor, and paralyzed, I thank Thee.

Ever since my first reading of Whitman I had held that this was his best; but I had no proof that he thought so till the other day. In order to picture him I had to read both his poetry and his prose through from beginning to end. His very last poem is "A Thought of Columbus," a greeting to him across the sea of time, soul-plaudits for him and acclamation of his great achievement. The very last page of his prose too, his final word and testament to his readers and to America is the confession of the same faith he put in the mouth of Columbus in the "Prayer" poem and is clothed in the self same words. It must be accepted then that the faith he attributes to Columbus is his own faith and the hope, his hope; he writes:

"The Highest said: 'Don't let us begin so low—isn't our range too coarse—too gross? . . . The Soul answered: No, not when we consider what it is all for—the end involved in Time and Space.

"Essentially my own printed records, all my volumes, are doubtless but off-hand utterances of my Personality, spontaneous, following implicitly the inscrutable command, dominated by that Personality, vaguely, even if decidedly, and with little or nothing of plan, art, erudition, etc. If I have chosen to hold the reins, the mastery, it has mainly been to give the way, the power, the road, to the invisible steeds."

"The potent felt interior command" of the great poem has become 'the inscrutable command' of the last page of his prose; his mission is from the Highest and he follows it implicitly.

It is curious that the metaphor he uses in the very last sentence has already been used magnificently by Goethe in his "Egmont." Whitman often reminds me of the great German. I ought to say that coming after Goethe he has borrowed from him, as I think he has in this instance. My readers shall judge. Goethe wrote:

"As if whipped by invisible Spirits the Sunhorses of Time have run away with the light car of our Destiny and nothing remains for us but with resolute hearts to hold fast the reins avoiding now the rock on the right, now the abyss on the left; whither we are speeding who can tell; hardly can we even remember whence we came!"

One more question remains to be answered: What is Whitman's position in the world of letters? Is he one of those who steer humanity and reveal unsuspected powers in human nature?

It seems to me that he is nearer akin to Browning than to any other English singer; but as soon as we think of them together Whitman's shortcomings and Whitman's noble attempt to reconcile Christianity and paganism declare themselves. Browning's "Rabbi ben Ezra" is as fine, I think, as Whitman's "Prayer to Columbus," and Browning has done several other things as good as the Rabbi. There are besides love-lyrics of the best in Browning and a hundred pictures of men and women from Andrea del Sarto to Bishop Blougram painted with intense vividness and reality. Browning has played critic very rarely, but whenever he does he use original insight and is most excellently educated to boot. His skill in words is not of the first order; but he is far above Whitman's crude provincialisms and ill-advised borrowings from imperfectly understood foreign tongues. Where it not for "The Prayer of Columbus," I should rate Poe almost as highly as the author of the "Leaves of Grass."

Yet I cannot leave Whitman on this note: he is boldly a pagan, and stands for the nobility of the flesh; yet the very spirit of Jesus is in him; somewhere in his prose he asks about a book: "Does it help the Soul?" and he recognizes, as Browning recognizes, that this is the all important question. Again and again Whitman speaks to the soul in its own language most nobly—encouraging it and is thereby fully and forever justified.

Even when singing of the body and its parts as sacred he says:

"O I say these are not the parts and poems of the body
    only, but of the soul,
O I say now these are the soul!"

| DATE DUE | | | |
|---|---|---|---|
| | | | |
| | | | |
| | | | |
| | | | |
| | | | |
| | | | |
| | | | |
| | | | |
| | | | |
| | | | |
| | | | |
| | | | |
| | | | |
| | | | |
| | | | |
| | | | |
| | | | |
| | | | |
| GAYLORD | | | PRINTED IN U.S.A. |